teach® yourself

quick fix
italian grammar

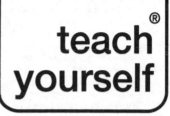

quick fix
italian grammar
vittoria bowles

For over 60 years, more than
40 million people have learnt over
750 subjects the **teach yourself**
way, with impressive results.

be where you want to be
with **teach yourself**

For UK order queries: please contact Bookpoint Ltd, 130 Milton Park, Abingdon, Oxon OX14 4TD. Telephone: +44 (0) 1235 827720, Fax: +44 (0) 1235 400454. Lines are open 9.00–18.00, Monday to Saturday, with a 24-hour message answering service. You can also order through our website www.madaboutbooks.com

For USA order queries: please contact McGraw-Hill Customer Services, P.O. Box 545, Blacklick, OH 43004-0545, USA. Telephone: 1-800-722-4726. Fax: 1-614-755-5645.

For Canada order queries: please contact McGraw-Hill Ryerson Ltd, 300 Water St, Whitby, Ontario L1N 9B6, Canada. Telephone: 905 430 5000. Fax: 905 430 5020.

Long renowned as the authoritative source for self-guided learning – with more than 30 million copies sold worldwide – the *Teach Yourself* series includes over 300 titles in the fields of languages, crafts, hobbies, business, computing and education.

British Library Cataloguing in Publication Data: a catalogue entry for this title is available from The British Library.

Library of Congress Catalog Card Number: on file

First published in UK 2003 by Hodder Headline Ltd, 338 Euston Road, London, NW1 3BH.

First published in US 2003 by Contemporary Books, a Division of the McGraw-Hill Companies, 1 Prudential Plaza, 130 East Randolph Street, Chicago, IL 60601 USA.

The 'Teach Yourself' name and logo are registered trade marks of Hodder & Stoughton Ltd.

Copyright © 2003 Vittoria Bowles
Advisory Editor: Sarah Butler

Typeset by Transet Limited, Coventry, England.
Printed in Great Britain for Hodder & Stoughton Educational, a division of Hodder Headline Ltd, 338 Euston Road, London NW1 3BH by Cox & Wyman Ltd, Reading, Berkshire.

Impression number	10 9 8 7 6 5 4 3 2 1
Year	2007 2006 2005 2004 2003

contents

Why learn a foreign language? Why Italian?

When you acquire the tool of communicating in another
language (in itself a useful practical achievement) you
enhance your personal development and self-assertion,
improve your attitude to and understanding of other people
and can expand your outlook on life in general. Italian is
the language closest to Latin, which has given the English
language very many of its words. This relationship will help
you greatly in reading and understanding Italian literature,
art and music. Further, because Italian is also a scientific
language it may be of great help to students of the physical
sciences and mathematics.

Techniques for learning

The process of learning a language is not always easy or
straightforward, and mastering the grammar of a second
language can be quite a challenge. One of the main reasons
that this grammar book has been developed is to give you
the opportunity of learning a few rules at a time, in a logical
sequence, and then immediately being able to practise them.
If you speak another language you have probably already
developed your own personal learning strategies. If you are
a newcomer you will need to discover the way which best
suits you. Remember that practice makes perfect: reading
and re-reading, writing and re-writing, saying and saying
again. Once you have acquired a basic structure you can try

modifying the sentences in the book by changing a noun, a verb or a gender, etc. to suit your own purposes. Verbs can be memorized by dividing them into groups with similar patterns. You can record them and listen to them wherever you can – in the car, in the bath, in bed.

How to use this book

You may consult this book in sequence, at random, or as a reference book, according to your needs. In general, the units are grouped progressively in grammar topics. The main rules of a topic, e.g. the genders of nouns, are immediately followed by more in-depth units. You can use the book in strict numerical sequence, although if you are a beginner you may wish to study the first one of two or more units of each grammar topic initially and then return to the more complex units as your proficiency increases. The exercises, placed immediately opposite the rules and at the back of the book, make it easy to refer back as needed to reinforce the points you are learning. Consult the Index as necessary to find the information you require, and the Glossary whenever you encounter an English term which you do not understand.

Buon divertimento e buon lavoro!

The author of *Teach Yourself Beginner's Italian* and *Teach Yourself Italian Vocabulary*, Vittoria Bowles has taught Italian for 27 years including 18 at the University of Brighton.

Sentences are made up of different elements: the most important of these are the subject and the verb.

A At least two elements are required for a sentence to make sense: a subject and a verb. For example, **Carla**, a noun, is the subject and **mangia** is a verb. **Carla mangia** (*Carla is eating*) is a whole expression with sufficient meaning to stand by itself.

Usually, though, more words go into a sentence: **Carla mangia una pesca** (*Carla is eating* (what?) *a peach*). **Una pesca** is called the complement (or object) because it illustrates the object of the action expressed by the verb (**mangiare**).

B Of course you could say or write something more complex like:

Carla mangia una pesca   *Carla is eating a peach*
   perché ha una gran fame   *because she is very hungry*
   e non ha nient'altro   *and she doesn't have anything*
   di commestibile in casa.   *else to eat in the house.*

This sentence is formed by several clauses: **Carla mangia una pesca** is the main clause since it can stand by itself; **perché ha una gran fame** and **e (perché) non ha nient'altro di commestibile in casa** are two dependent clauses since they can't stand by themselves.

C Traditionally speech contains nine parts:

1 Article: **il, lo, la, l', i, gli, le** (*the*); **un, uno, una, un'** (*a/an*)
2 Noun or name of things, animals and people: **strada** (*road*), **gatto** (*cat*), **Maria, bellezza** (*beauty*).

3 Adjective: **buono** (*good*), **chiaro** (*clear*), **intelligente** (*intelligent*).
4 Pronoun: **io** (*I*), **mi** (*me*), **lo** (*it/him*), **gli** (*to him*), **il mio** (*my*), **questo** (*this*).
5 Verb: **parlare** (*to speak*), **vedere** (*to see*), **partire** (*to leave/depart*).
6 Adverb: **lentamente** (*slowly*), **bene** (*well*), **presto** (*soon/early*).
7 Preposition: **di** (*of*), **a** (*to/at*), **per** (*for*), **dopo** (*after*), **vicino a** (*near*).
8 Conjunction: **e** (*and*), **anche** (*also*), **oppure** (*or*), **perché** (*because/why*).
9 Interjection: **ahimè!** (*alas!*), **ahi!** (*ouch!*), **coraggio!** (*take heart!*).

Of these nine, the following five are variable or have variable endings which agree in gender and number with the subject: article, noun, adjective, pronoun and verb. The other four (adverb, preposition, conjunction and interjection/ exclamation) are usually invariable, that is they do not undergo any change.

exercise

Put the words below into the right order to form two sentences:

a una / banana / mangia / Maria
b Paolo / pizza / una / mangia / fame / perché / ha

The order of words in Italian sentences can differ greatly from that of English sentences.

A In Italian, the grammatical form of words, including their appropriate endings, is very important, whereas the actual order of words is less so. The subject, for example, can be placed almost anywhere in the sentence. *Tomorrow Renza is going to Sori* can be translated as: **Domani Renza va a Sori; Renza va a Sori domani; Va a Sori domani Renza; A Sori va domani Renza.** The difference in meaning is in the change of emphasis.

B Subject pronouns **io** (*I*), **tu** (*you*), etc. are omitted except when needed for emphasis: **Esco** (*I am going out*), **Io esco** (*I am going out*). When placed after the verb, the emphasis is even greater: **Esco io** (*I (not you) am going out*).

C To make a question in Italian, you don't need to alter the order of the words: a question mark at the end of the sentence suffices:

   Costa caro. *It is expensive.*   Costa caro? *Is it expensive?*

D The negative form requires only a **non** before the verb.
   Non costa molto.   *It doesn't cost much.*

Do, did, does, etc. in questions or the negative are NEVER translated.

E Adjectives generally follow the noun but not necessarily (see Unit 18). You can say:

Angelo vive in una casa grande.   *Angelo lives in a large house.*
Angelo vive in una grande casa.

In the former example, the emphasis falls on the adjective **grande**.

F The position of adverbs is usually before the adjective, if there is one ...

Paolo è un bambino molto vivace. *Paul is a very lively boy.*
... and after the verb:

Il martedì vado sempre   *On Tuesdays I always go*
 a Brighton.   *to Brighton.*

With compound tenses, adverbs of time (e.g. **sempre** (*always*)) are placed between the auxiliary verb and the past participle, as in English:

Non sono mai stata a Roma. *I have never been to Rome.*

exercise

Put the sentences below into the interrogative and negative forms.

E.g. Devo finire. (*I must finish.*) → Devo finire? Non devo finire.

a Posso andare. (*I can/may go.*)
b Posso parlare. (*I can/may speak.*)
c Devo pagare il conto. (*I must pay the bill.*)
d Devo scrivere la lettera. (*I must write the letter.*)
e Devo leggere questo libro. (*I must read this book.*)

The Italian alphabet consists of 21 letters: a, b, c, d, e, f, g, h, i, l, m, n, o, p, q, r, s, t, u, v and z.

The other five letters (j, k, w, x, y) are used to write words of classical or foreign origin, e.g. **xilofono** (*xylophone*), **box** (*lock-up garage*).

A In Italian, some words carry an accent on the last letter. It may be either grave (è) or acute (é): **qualità** (*quality*), **più** (*more/plus*), **è** (*s/he/it is*), **perché** (*why/because*). The grave accent is used at the end of those words which are pronounced with an open -e (as in 'red') such as: **caffè** (*coffee*), **tè** (*tea*), **cioè** (*that is (to say)*). Acute accents go on words pronounced with a closed -e (as in 'they') at the end: **perché** (*why/because*), **sé** (*oneself*), **né** (*neither*), **benché** (*although*), **poiché** (*since*).

B When two vowels come together, at the end of one word and the beginning of the next, the final vowel of the first word is replaced with an apostrophe ('). This is compulsory with the articles **lo**, **la** and **una** and with combined prepositions and articles.

l'amico *the friend*   l'ala *the wing*   un'arancia *an orange*
nell(o)'orto *in the vegetable garden*
dell(o)'ortolano *of the greengrocer*
sull(a)'altalena *on the swing*   dall(o)'arco *from the arch*

Often **di** is also treated this way: **d'inverno** (*in winter*), **d'argento** (*in silver*).

C Other expressions which take an apostrophe are:

d'ora in poi	*from now on*
senz'altro	*without any doubt*
nient'altro	*nothing else*
tutt'altro	*on the contrary*

In most other cases it is either strictly forbidden (e.g. with the article **le** = **le erbe**) or only optional and thus avoidable (**gli italiani**).

exercises

Write the appropriate accents on the last vowels of these words:

a ne b e c benche d se e cioe f perche
g poiche h te

Use an apostrophe with the pairs of words below if appropriate.

E.g. la elica (*propeller*) → l'elica.

i lo zero (*zero*) j di estate (*in summer*) k dallo autobus (*from the bus*) l di oro (*in gold*) m un problema (*problem*) n una arancia (*orange*) o una amica (*friend*) p un aereo (*plane*) q una ala (*wing*)

Sometimes in Italian a vowel or even a whole syllable is lost at the end of a word.

A The loss of a vowel – or sometimes a whole syllable – can occur at the end of a word without the use of an apostrophe. With words ending in -re, -ne, -le and -ra, -na, -la, it is optional and used only to produce a better sound:

mal(e) di gola *sore throat*   cuor(e) di leone *lion heart*

B The apostrophe occurs only before a vowel, whereas a shortened word can also occur before a consonant (except -z, gn, -ps, -x or -s followed by another consonant).

C Signore (*Sir/Mr*), professore (*teacher/professor*), dottore (*doctor*), ingegnere (*civil/naval engineer*) always lose their final vowel when followed by a surname.

il signor Cervi *Mr Cervi*   il professor Neri *Professor Neri*

D Infinitives can also be shortened, particularly before another infinitive.

poter andare *to be able to go*   lavorar sodo *to work hard*

E Quello (*that*), bello (*beautiful*), grande (*large/great*), santo (*saint*) are shortened before a word beginning with a consonant.

quel libro è mio *that is my book* un bel bambino *a beautiful child*

They take an apostrophe before a vowel: quell'uomo *that man*

Also **quale** often drops the final -e: Qual è …? *Which is …?*

Similarly, **buono** (*good*), **uno** (*one/a/an*), **alcuno** (*any*) and **nessuno** (*nobody/no/not any*), drop their final vowel.

un buon amico *a good friend*   nessun uomo *no man*

F Generally words are not shortened in the plural: buoni amici *good friends*.

G There are a few cases where a word which has lost its last vowel or syllable does use an apostrophe, irrespective of the following word: **po'** = **poco** (*little*), **mo'** = **modo** (*way/manner*), plus the imperatives **da'** = **dai** (*give!*), **sta'** = **stai** (*stay!*), **di'** = **dici** (*say!*), **va'** = **vai** (*go!*), **fa'** = **fai** (*do (it)!*), **to'** = **tieni** (*take!*).

H There are two very short words, **a** (*to/at*) and **e** (*and*), which, before a word starting with a vowel, take a **-d**. This makes them sound better:

Renza va ad Asti	*Renza is going to Asti*
Marco ed Elisa	*Marco and Elisa*

exercise

Translate the following into Italian.

E.g. a beautiful child → un bel bambino

a a friend
b a good friend
c that man
d Which is ...?
e good friends
f to be able to go

g no friends
h to work hard
i that book
j take!
k Mr Cervi
l Doctor Green

Words for people, animals, places, objects or concepts are called nouns. All Italian nouns have a gender.

A Italian nouns are either masculine or feminine and, except for a few Latin words or words of foreign origin such as **bar**, **film** and **album**, which are mostly masculine, they end in -o, -a or -e.

Most nouns ending in -o are masculine: **uomo** (*man*); **cavallo** (*horse*); **bambino** (*little boy*); **ragazzo** (*boy*); **aeroplano** (*airplane*); **treno** (*train*); **orario** (*timetable*); **oro** (*gold*).

Most nouns ending in **-a** are feminine: **donna** (*woman*); **bambina** (*little girl*); **ragazza** (*girl*); **casa** (*house/home*); **banca** (*bank*); **commedia** (*play/comedy*).

Nouns ending in -e can be either masculine or feminine. The dictionary will give you the gender; next to the noun you will find s.m. (= sostantivo maschile) for the masculine form and s.f. (= sostantivo femminile) for the feminine one: **carne** (s.f.) *meat*; **cane** (s.m.) *dog*; **colore** (s.m.) *colour*

B Some nouns do not follow the above rule.

> *Masculine*
> clima; pigiama; programma; telegramma; tema; diploma; problema; profeta; sistema; poeta; pianeta; duca; dramma; papa; vaglia; cinema(tografo)
> *Feminine*
> mano; radio; dinamo; crisi; auto(mobile); moto(cicletta); foto(grafia); eco

C Most often masculine nouns referring to people change their -o ending into an -a to form the feminine: **zio/zia** (*uncle-aunt*); **cittadino/cittadina** (*citizen*). The dictionary gives the masculine form of such nouns, followed by -a (or other suffix) to indicate its feminine equivalent.

D Nouns ending in -tore form the feminine with -trice: **attore/attrice** (*actor/actress*), **pittore/pittrice** (*painter*), BUT **dottore/dottoressa** (*doctor*).

E Masculine nouns ending in -e form the feminine in two ways: some change the -e into -a: **infermiere/infermiera** (*nurse*); **cameriere/cameriera** (*waiter/tress*); others, usually those indicating profession or title, change the -e into -essa: **professore/professoressa** (*lecturer*); **dottore/dottoressa** (*doctor*). In spite of this rule, academic, office, rank and many professional titles are more often used in the masculine form: **l'ambasciatore Signora** … (*the (female) ambassador*), **il sindaco Signora** … (*the mayoress*).

exercise

Some of the words above have not been translated. Without the help of the dictionary, match the words below to their Italian equivalent and give their gender.

a programme	f	aunt
b radio	g	poet
c problem	h	theme
d photo	i	motorbike
e climate		

In English, the plural is mainly formed by adding an -s to the singular form: *boy-boys*. **Italian does it in a different way.**

A Masculine nouns (ending in -o or -a) form their plural with -i.
bambino → bambini (*children*); problema → problemi (*problems*)
BUT uomo → uomini (*men*)

B Feminine nouns ending in -a form their plural with -e:
mamma → mamme (*mums*); scatola → scatole (*boxes*); gonna →
gonne (*skirts*)

C Nouns ending in -e (masculine and feminine) form their
plural with -i.
luce → luci (*lights*); fiore → fiori (*flowers*)

D Nouns ending in -co, -go, -ca and -ga do not always behave
in the same way but usually acquire an -h between the -c/-g and
the ending (-i or -e).
buco → buchi (*holes*); fungo → funghi (*mushrooms*);
banca → banche; (*banks*); diga → dighe (*dams/dykes*)

Nouns ending in -ico (NOT -ica) follow the normal masculine rule.
medico → medici (*doctors*); sindaco → sindaci (*mayors*); amico
→ amici (*friends*); nemico → nemici (*enemies*); greco → greci
(*Greeks*); porco → porci (*pigs*); farmaco → farmaci (*medicines*);
stomaco → stomaci (*stomachs*); monaco → monaci (*monks*)

E Nouns ending in accented vowels do not change in the plural.
città (*city, cities/town, towns*); qualità (*quality, qualities*);
virtù (*virtue(s)*); caffè (*coffee(s)*)

F Nouns ending in **-io**, where the stress falls on the -i (there are not many), have a regular plural by changing the -o into an -i: zio → zii (*uncles*).

All the others just lose the -o:

viaggio → viaggi (*trips*), figlio → figli (*sons*)

G Words ending in **-cia** and **-gia** tend to form their plural in one of two ways. If -c and -g are preceded by a vowel, they usually keep the -i and add an -e:

camicia → camicie (*shirts*), valigia → valigie (*or* valige) (*suitcases*)

If preceded by a consonant, they lose the -i and add an -e:

spiaggia → spiagge (*beaches*).

In Italian **euro** (*euro*) doesn't change in the plural:

1 euro → 10 euro

exercise

Write the singular form of the nouns below.

E.g. dighe → diga

a fiori	g banche
b bambini	h luci
c problemi	i strade
d uomini	j borse
e mamme	k funghi
f gonne	l scatole

Several words translate *the* in Italian. These vary according to the gender, number and the first letter of the following nouns.

	masculine	feminine
singular	il ragazzo lo zero l'aereo	la ragazza l'arancia
plural	i ragazzi gli zeri gli aerei	le ragazze le arance

A The article **il** precedes the majority of singular masculine nouns:

il libro (*the book*); il problema (*the problem*);
il fiore (*the flower*)

Its plural form is **i**:

i libri (*the books*); i problemi (*the problems*);
i fiori (*the flowers*)

B However, **lo** precedes masculine nouns starting with:
• **s** followed by consonant: lo specchio (*mirror*); lo sci (*ski*)
• **z**: lo zucchero (*sugar*), lo zero (*zero*), lo zio (*uncle*)
• **x**: lo xilofono (*xylophone*), lo xenofobo (*xenophobe*)
• **pn, ps**: lo pneumatico (*pneumatic/tyre*)*; lo psicologo (*psychologist*)
• **gn, sc**: lo gnocco (*dumpling*); lo sciopero (*strike*); lo sceicco (*sheik*)
• **i** followed by another vowel: lo ione (*ion*).

*You will, however, often hear **il pneumatico** → **i pneumatici**

C Before masculine nouns starting with a vowel the form **l'** is used: l'aereo (*plane*); l'elicottero (*helicopter*)

D **Lo** is used instead of **il** in adverbial expressions like **per lo più** (*mostly*) and **per lo meno** (*at least*).

E The plural form of **lo** and **l'** is **gli**. **Gli** can become **gl'** before a noun starting with **i-** but the whole form is better:
gli studenti (*students*); gli zeri (*zeros*); gli xenofobi (*xenophobes*); gli pseudonimi (*pseudonyms*); gli scioperi (*strikes*); gli aerei (*planes*); gli elicotteri (*helicopters*); gli Italiani (*Italians*)

Gli is also used instead of **i** before **dei** (*gods*): gli dei.

F The feminine article is **la**: la giacca (*jacket*); la borsa (*bag*). **La**, before a noun starting with a vowel, like **lo** above, becomes **l'**: l'isola (*island*); l'arancia (*orange*); l'auto (*car*). The plural form of **la** or **l'** is **le**: le signore (*ladies*); le cravatte (*ties*). **Le** NEVER becomes **l'**: le ore (*hours*); le unghie (*finger nails*).

exercise

Write the definite article before the following nouns.

E.g. elicottero → l'elicottero

a	_____ gnocco	g	_____ auto
b	_____ casa	h	_____ sci
c	_____ aereo	i	_____ arancia
d	_____ sciopero	j	_____ specchio
e	_____ psicologo	k	_____ problema
f	_____ xenofobo		

The definite article is not always used as in English.

The definite article (*the*) is used in the following cases:

A Geographical names such as continents, countries, regions, counties, large islands, lakes, mountains:

l'Europa (*Europe*); l'Italia (*Italy*); la Toscana (*Tuscany*); il Kent (*Kent*); la Cornovaglia (*Cornwall*); la Sicilia (*Sicily*); il Monte Bianco (*Mont Blanc*).

After the preposition *in*, the article is omitted provided it is not qualified by an adjective or an adjectival phrase.

Abito in Inghilterra.	*I live in England.*
Vado in Spagna.	*I am going to Spain.*

BUT

nell' (in+l') Inghilterra di Cromwell	*in Cromwell's England*
nell'Italia Meridionale	*in Southern Italy*

B Titles: il duca d'Aosta (*the duke of Aosta*); il dottor Neri (*Dr Neri*); il signor/la signora Verdi (*Mr/Mrs Verdi*).

C Women's surnames:

La Loren è molto ammirata.	*Loren is much admired.*

D Expressions of time and dates:

Sono le tre.	*It's three o'clock.*
Lavoro dalle (da + le) nove alle (a + le) cinque.	*I work from nine to five.*

BUT

È mezzogiorno/mezzanotte.	*It is midday/midnight.*

Il 1993 è stato un anno molto bello.   *1993 was a lovely year.*
Mario è nato nel (in + il) 1966.   *Mario was born in 1966.*

E Names of languages, except with the verb **parlare**:
Francesca studia il cinese.   *Francesca studies Chinese.*
Parla inglese?   *Do you speak English?*

F Parts of the body, clothes and objects we own, such as cars. In these cases Italian uses the definite article rather than the possessive adjective:
Mi lavo le mani.   *I am washing my hands.*
Vado a prendere la macchina.   *I am going to get my car.*

G Nouns used in a 'general' sense:
Amo la musica.   *I love music.*
I gatti sono indipendenti.   *Cats are independent.*

H Expressions such as **tutti e due**, **ambedue**, **entrambi** (*both*):
tutti e due/ambedue/entrambi i bambini   *both children*

exercise

Write the definite article where required.

a ___ Cina
b ___ Francia
c ___ Inghilterra
d ___ signora Rossi
e ___ signor Bianchi
f Mi piacciono (*I like*) ___ spaghetti.
g Abito ___ Toscana.
h Sean Connery è nato in ___ Scozia?
i È ___ Sean Connery!
j È ___ Loren!

Here are some more cases in which the definite article is used in Italian but not in English.

Italian uses the definite article in the following situations:

A With prices, weights, measures and other figures such as percentages.

Questo vino costa quattro euro e 50 al (a + il) litro.	*This wine costs 4 euros 50 per litre.*
il 30% della popolazione	*30% of the population*
Una lezione costa 25 sterline all' (a + l')ora.	*A lesson costs £25 per hour.*
Il prezzo è aumentato del (di + il) dieci per cento.	*The price has increased by 10%.*

B With names of towns when accompanied by an adjective or adjectival phrase.

la Firenze del (di + il) Cinquecento	*Florence of the 16th century*

C With certain expressions.

Mi piace vedere/guardare la televisione.	*I like watching television.*
Che cosa c'è alla televisione?	*What is on television?*
A che ora è la colazione/il pranzo/la cena?	*What time is breakfast/lunch/ dinner?*

D *The* is not translated with expressions like *to/in the mountains, to/in the office, to/in the country, in the car.*

Vado in montagna ogni anno.	*I go to the mountains every year.*
Abito in campagna.	*I live in the country.*
Vado/Sono in ufficio alle otto.	*I go to/am in the office at eight.*
Vado/Sono in piscina.	*I am going to/I am in the swimming pool.*

E The definite article is also used with the preposition **di** (*of*) to translate *some* and *any*. In this case its function is to indicate a part of something or an unspecified quantity.

| Ho delle (di + le) mele. | *I have some apples.* |
| Ha delle mele? | *Have you any apples?* |

exercise

Use the information above to help you find the answers to these questions:

a Quanto costa al litro questo vino?
b Quanto costa una lezione all'ora?
c Di quanto è aumentato il prezzo?
d Quando vai in montagna?
e Che cosa ti piace fare?
f Dove abiti?
g A che ora vai in ufficio?

The indefinite article is used for non-specified nouns, that is, *a friend* as opposed to *the friend*. In Italian it has four forms: *un, uno, un'* and *una*.

A **Un** precedes masculine nouns: un amico (*a friend*); un attore (*an actor*).

It becomes **uno** before s followed by a consonant, before z, x, gn, ps or pn, and before i followed by another vowel: uno spreco (*a waste*); uno zoo (*a zoo*); uno gnocco (*a dumpling*); uno sci (*a ski*); uno ione (*an ion*); uno psicologo (*a psicologist*).

B The feminine form is **una**: una mela (*an apple*); una pentola (*a saucepan*); una pagina (*a page*)

Una becomes **un'** before a vowel: un'arancia (*an orange*); un'ala (*a wing*); un'attrice (*an actress*)
BUT una iena (*a hyena*).

Remember that the masculine form **un** NEVER takes an apostrophe.

The numeral **uno** (*one*) is the same word as the indefinite article. It therefore agrees in gender with the noun and takes the same forms as above: un uomo (*one man*); uno sci (*one ski*); una casa (*one house*); un'ape (*one bee*)

C The indefinite article doesn't have a plural. There are, however, forms for *some* and *any*.

exercises

Write the indefinite article before the following nouns.

E.g. quadro → un quadro

a _____ attore

b _____ amico

c _____ cane

d _____ gatto

e _____ gnocco

f _____ sci

g _____ zero

h _____ psicologo

i _____ xenofobo

j _____ mela

k _____ pentola

l _____ pagina

m _____ ala

n _____ attrice

o _____ iena

p _____ pagina

q _____ ape

r _____ zoo

What are these?

Un and una, etc. are used less in Italian than a and an in English.

The indefinite article is not translated in the following cases:

A When a role, job, profession, nationality or religion is preceded by **essere** (*to be*) or **diventare** (*to become*) …
Alberto è/è diventato avvocato. *Albert is/has become a lawyer.*
Cristina è cattolica.   *Cristina is a Catholic.*

… unless qualified by an adjective or followed by an object:
Anna è una segretaria   *Anna is an efficient*
  efficiente.   *secretary.*
Sono un impiegato delle poste. *I am a Post Office worker.*

B With expressions starting **Che …** (*What a …*):
Che bel ragazzo!   *What a handsome young man!*
Che peccato!   *What a pity!*

C Before **cento** (*hundred*), **mille** (*thousand*), **mezzo/a** (*half*):
Te l'ho detto mille volte!   *I've told you a thousand times!*
mezz'ora   *half an hour*
mezzo litro di latte   *half a litre of milk*

D However, when *a/an* stands for *every/per*, it is translated by **a** + definite article:
Vado in Italia due volte all'anno. *I go to Italy twice a year.*
Insegno sei ore al giorno.   *I teach six hours a/per day.*

E Note these expressions with **avere/prendere** (*to have/catch*):
avere … (il) mal di gola *a sore throat*; … (il) mal di denti

a toothache; … (il) mal di testa *a headache*; … il raffreddore *a cold*; … appetito *an appetite*
prendere … il mal di gola; … il raffreddore
Also: avere l'automobile (*to have a car*); avere fretta (*to be in a hurry*).

F The indefinite article can be used in Italian for emphasis to express words like *such a …* or when a noun is followed by an adjective:

Aveva una fretta!	*He was in such a hurry!*
Ho un raffreddore terribile.	*I have a terrible cold.*

G **Da** is used instead of *as a* in the following kind of expressions:

Mio figlio studia da interprete. *My son is studying as an interpreter.*
Da bambina ero un maschiaccio. *As a child I was a tomboy.*

exercise

Add the indefinite article when needed.

E.g. Cristina è _____ segretaria diligente. → Cristina è una segretaria diligente.

a Alberto è _____ dottore.
b Francesco è _____ segretario.
c Mariangela è _____ professoressa universitaria.
d Cesare è _____ avvocato famoso.
e Umberto è _____ avvocato di successo (*successful*).
f Emanuela è _____ cattolica.

Some nouns seem to have two genders but they are actually different words with different meanings.

The distinction between masculine and feminine nouns makes sense only for those nouns referring to people and animals. The gender of nouns referring to things is purely a grammatical convention since it is obvious that objects are neither male or female. You will need to learn the different meanings of these nouns, some of which differ only in their gender, some of which differ in gender and ending.

MASCULINE	FEMININE
l'arco (*arch*)	l'arca (*ark*)
il boa (*boa (snake)*)	la boa (*buoy*)
il camerata (*comrade*)	la camerata (*dormitory*)
il capitale (*capital (money)*)	la capitale (*capital (city)*)
il colpo (*blow*)	la colpa (*fault/guilt*)
il collo (*neck*)	la colla (*glue*)
il fonte (*font (in a church)*)	la fonte (*spring (water source)*)
il foglio (*sheet (page)*)	la foglia (*leaf*)
il fosso (*ditch/moat*)	la fossa (*pit/hole*)

il fine (*aim/purpose*)   la fine (*end*)
il manico (*handle*)   la manica (*sleeve/English Channel*)
il modo (*way/manner*)   la moda (*fashion*)
il mostro (*monster*)   la mostra (*exhibition*)
il panno (*cloth*)   la panna (*cream*)
il pianto (*crying/tears*)   la pianta (*plant/plan/map*)
il posto (*place*)   la posta (*post/mail*)
il radio (*radius/radium*)   la radio (*radio*)
il tappo (*cork/plug*)   la tappa (*stage/leg/lap*)
il tasso (*rate/yew/badger*)   la tassa (*tax/fee/duty*)
il visto (*visa/tick/check*)   la vista (*sight/view*)

exercise

Write the nouns for these objects (definite article + noun).

Some nouns referring to people have only one form, and the gender of the person can be recognized by the article or the following adjective.

Nouns with only one form (called 'nouns of common gender') include:

A Nouns ending in -ista and -cida
il/la farmacista (*chemist*); un/un'artista (*artist*);
il/la violinista (*violinist*); il/la suicida (*suicide*)

B Some nouns of Greek origin ending in -a:
il/la collega (*colleague*); il/la pediatra (*paediatrician*);
l'atleta (*athlete*)

The plural forms of the above nouns follow the normal plural pattern.
il farmacista → i farmacisti; la farmacista → le farmaciste
il collega → i colleghi; la collega → le colleghe

C Some nouns ending in -e:
il/la nipote (*grandchild/nephew/niece*); il/la parente
(*relative*); il/la consorte (*spouse*); il/la cantante (*singer*);
un/un'insegnante (*teacher*): un/un'amante (*lover*)

These nouns ending in -e have an identical plural form for both the masculine and the feminine.
il cantante → i cantanti; la cantante → le cantanti

D Nouns like persona (*person*); guida (*guide*); guardia (*guard*) and polizia (*police*) where feminine nouns are applied to either gender:

Quell'uomo è una persona intelligente.

That man is an intelligent person.

Il marito è una guida turistica.

The husband is a tourist guide.

Remember that nouns ending with an accented vowel have only one form: la città → le città (see Unit 6).

E Some nouns for animals have a male and female form: cavallo (*stallion*), cavalla (*mare*); cervo (*stag*), cerva (*hind*); bufalo (*bull buffalo*), bufala (*cow buffalo*).

However, the majority of nouns for animals only have one gender and thus need to be followed by **maschio** or **femmina** to indicate the animal's sex.

la volpe maschio *or* il maschio della volpe *dog-fox*
il leopardo femmina *or* la femmina del leopardo *female leopard*

exercise

Add the feminine form to the list of nouns below and give their plural forms.

E.g. il farmacista → i farmacisti; la farmacista → le farmaciste; il cantante → i cantanti; la cantante → le cantanti

a il ciclista (*cyclist*)
b il turista (*tourist*)
c il violinista (*violinist*)
d l'arpista (*harpist*)
e il pianista (*pianist*)
f il collega (*colleague*)
g l'atleta (*athlete*)
h il pediatra (*paediatrician*)
i lo psichiatra (*psychiatrist*)
j lo stratega (*strategist*)

14 gender (4); plural (2)

Some masculine nouns have a slightly different feminine form and some have a completely different one; others have no plural or no singular form.

A Among the nouns with an irregular feminine form are: eroe/eroina (*hero/ heroine*); dio/dea (*god/goddess*); re/regina (*king/queen*); cane/cagna (*dog/bitch*)

B Among masculine nouns with a completely different feminine form are: uomo/donna (*man/woman*); padre/madre (*father/mother*); babbo (*or* papà)/mamma (*dad/mum*); marito/moglie (*husband/wife*); fratello/sorella (*brother/sister*); genero/nuora (*son/daughter-in-law*); celibe (*or* scapolo)/ nubile (*bachelor/single* or *unmarried*); maschio/femmina (*male/female*)

C Some nouns keep the same ending in both the singular and plural:
- those ending in an accented vowel: bontà
- those ending in -i: tesi, brindisi, analisi
- nouns formed with only one syllable such as **re** and **gru**
- feminine nouns ending in -ie: serie, specie (BUT moglie → mogli)
- some masculine nouns ending in -a: gorilla, sosia, lama, cinema
- some feminine nouns ending in -o: dinamo, radio, auto, foto
- nouns ending in a consonant: autobus, gas, bar, film, album, tram

D Some have no singular form: le forbici (*scissors*); gli occhiali (*glasses*); le nozze (*marriage/wedding*); i pantaloni/calzoni (*trousers*)

E Some nouns have no plural form.
• most metals: il rame (*copper*); l'argento (*silver*)
• la fame (*hunger*); la sete (*thirst*); l'uva (*grapes*); la prole (*offspring*)
• groups of people, animals or things:
  un branco (*pack*); la folla (*crowd*); la gente (*people*); il gregge (*flock (sheep)*); la mandria (*herd*); la polizia (*police*); il consiglio comunale (*town council*); la marina (*navy*); l'aviazione (*airforce*)
In English one often says: *'The police are ...'*, *'The council are ...'*; this is not the case in Italian. Unless you are talking about various groups of people or more than one council you say: **La gente è ...** (*The people is ...*).

exercise

Write the plural form of the following nouns and articles.

E.g. la tesi → le tesi

a la metropoli	**i** la serie (*series*)	**q** la moglie (*wife*)
b il brindisi	**j** la specie (*species*)	**r** il cinema
c l'analisi (f)	**k** l'auto (f)	**s** l'autobus (m)
d l'ipotesi (f)	**l** la gru (*crane*)	**t** il gas
e l'oasi (f)	**m** la radio (*radio*)	**u** il bar
f la bontà	**n** il sosia (*one's double*)	**v** il film
g la foto	**o** la dinamo (*dynamo*)	**w** l'album (m)
h il re (*king*)	**p** il lama (*llama*)	**x** il tram

Certain masculine nouns ending in -o form their plural with -a and become feminine in the process.

A Many of these gender-changing nouns relate to numbers or measurements.

un miglio (*one mile*)
due miglia (*two miles*)
un centinaio (*about one hundred*)
molte centinaia (*many hundreds*)
un migliaio (*about one thousand*)
alcune migliaia (*some thousands*)
un dito (*one finger*)
due dita (*two fingers*)

B In this category also belong a group of masculine words which, while having a feminine plural ending in **-a**, also have a regular plural ending in **-i** with a different meaning.

il braccio (*arm/beam*)   i bracci (*arms of a chandelier/scales*)
le braccia (*of the human body*)

il corno (*horn*)   i corni (*horns = musical instrument*)
le corna (*horns of animals*)

il membro (*member/limb*)   i membri (*members of a club or commission*)
le membra (*members = limbs of the human body*)

il muro (*wall*)   i muri (*walls of a house*)
le mura (*walls of a city or a fortress*)

l'osso (*bone*)   gli ossi (*bones, mainly of animals*
                                              (i.e. for the dog))
                                          le ossa (*human bones*)

C Observe these words:
 il frutto/i frutti (*fruits while on a plant or a tree*)
 la frutta/le frutta (*fruits after they have been picked*)
 il legno/i legni (*wood of a tree/furniture*)
 la legna/le legna (*wood for burning*)

exercise

Crossword

ACROSS
3 The walls of a house.
4 Parts of the human body joined to the shoulders.
5 Parts of the human body.
6 Fido buries them.

DOWN
1 The members of a club.
2 The arms of a chandelier.
5 City walls.
7 The bones in the human body.

Endings like *-ino*, *-etto*, etc. qualify the noun in the same way as an adjective does.

Observe these nouns:
casa   casina/casetta   casona   casaccia   casuccia

A **Casina** means *small house*. The ending **-ino** (**-ina** in the feminine) can be used instead of **piccolo** (*small*). **-etto** and **-ello**, as well as **-uzzo**, **-icino**, **-olino** and **-erello**, are other endings that can be used in the same way:
   libretto (*small book*); **fuocherello*** (*small fire*); **bambinello** (*little child*); **ossicino** (*small bone*); **labbruzzo** (*small lip*).
All these endings have regular feminine and plural forms. They are added after dropping the final vowel of the root word. While not applied to all nouns, these endings are in common usage and are often heard.

*Root words ending in **-ca**, **-ga**, **-co**, **-go** follow the same rule as for the formation of the plural (Unit 6D).

B **Casona** means *large house*. **-one** (**-ona** in the feminine) stands for **grande** (*large*) or **forte** (*strong*)
   un librone (*a large book*)

The ending **-one** can also be applied to feminine nouns, in which case they become masculine:
   una bottiglia (*a bottle*) → **un bottiglione** (*a large bottle*)
   una donna (*a woman*) → **un donnone** (*a tall, large woman*)

C **Casaccia** means *ugly house*. So **-accio/-accia** stand for *ugly*, *hateful*, *despicable* and similar:
 una donnaccia (*a despicable woman*)

D **Casuccia** stands for *nice, pretty little house*. **-uccio/-uccia** are terms of endearment and stand for *small, nice, pretty*.

E The value of these endings very much depends on the mood of the person using them. For example, **babbino**, said by a child, is not a small dad, but a dear one; **poveraccio** doesn't mean a poor bad man but a poor old soul.

F Do not confuse this class of nouns with ordinary nouns ending in the same way such as **bottone** (*button*), **limone** (*lemon*) or **bottino** (*booty*).

Names of people can also undergo the same kind of modification: Giuseppe → Giuseppino, Pino, Pinuccio, Pinotto, Peppino, Beppe, Beppone, Peppone, Pippo.

exercise

Pair the nouns on the left with their altered terms on the right.

a tavolo	f carta	1 cartaccia	6 dentone
b tesoro	g uomo	2 tavolino	7 bastoncino
c pacco	h bastone	3 elefantino	8 pacchetto
d prato	i dente	4 praticello	9 squadretta
e squadra	j elefante	5 tesoruccio	10 ometto/omino

Compound nouns are those formed by two words: for example *la banconota* (banknote) is formed from *banco* (bank) and *nota* (note).

A The majority of these nouns form their plurals like other nouns:
   il francobollo → i francobolli (*stamps*)
   il passaporto → i passaporti (*passports*)

B Where the compound noun is formed by one of the following constructions, both components change into the plural:
   noun + adjective: il fabbroferraio (*blacksmith*) → i fabbriferrai
   noun + past participle: la terracotta (*earthenware*) → le terrecotte

However, in the case of the following constructions, both components stay unchanged:
   verb + verb   il saliscendi (*going up and down/latch*)
                          → i saliscendi
   adverb + verb il benestare (*approval*) → i benestare
   verb + adverb il posapiano (*slowcoach*) → i posapiano
   verb + noun   il cavalcavia (*flyover*) → i cavalcavia

C No rules apply in the case of compound nouns formed with the word **capo**. When in doubt consult the dictionary:
   il caposquadra → i capisquadra (*foremen/military squads/*
                                           leaders)/sports captains)
   il capoverso → i capoversi   (*paragraphs/indentations*)
   il capotecnico → i capitecnici (*chief technicians*)
   il capostazione → i capistazione (*station-masters*)

il capogiro → i capogiri   (*dizzy spells*)
il capofila → i capifila   (*leaders (of a file or line)*)
il capolavoro → i capolavori   (*masterpieces*)
il capogruppo → i capigruppo   (*group leaders*)

exercise

Crossword

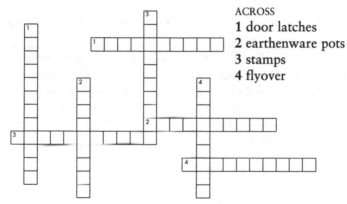

ACROSS
1 door latches
2 earthenware pots
3 stamps
4 flyover

DOWN
1 blacksmiths
2 banknotes
3 passports
4 approvals

These are words that add a quality or a specification to a noun.

A Descriptive adjectives usually agree in gender and number with the noun they qualify, and they usually follow it.

	singular	plural
Masculine	-o **un uomo onesto** *an honest man*	-i **due uomini onesti** *two honest men*
Feminine	-a **una ragazza onesta** *an honest girl*	-e **due ragazze oneste** *two honest girls*
Masculine and Feminine	-e **un vestito semplice** *a simple dress* **una casa grande** *a large house*	-i **due vestiti semplici** *two simple dresses* **due case grandi** *two large houses*

B Adjectives ending in **-e** maintain the **-e** for both the masculine and feminine singular, changing to an **-i** in the plural:
Paul è inglese. Anna è danese.   Paul e Linda sono inglesi.

C Where there are two or more nouns of different genders, adjectives take the masculine ending since this has a more 'neutral' value than the feminine form.
Mario e Giulia sono italiani.   *Mario and Giulia are Italian.*

D Some adjectives can be placed either before or after the noun but this can slightly or significantly alter their meaning.

Both **un libro vecchio** and **un vecchio libro** mean *an old book* but in the former case the emphasis is on *old*.

un vecchio amico (*an old friend*), un amico vecchio (*a friend who is old*); un uomo povero (*a man who is poor*), un pover'uomo (*a poor old soul*); un grand'uomo (*a great man*), un uomo grande (*a large man*)

E Colours follow the noun:

una macchina verde   *a green car*

F When two adjectives describe a noun, one is usually put before and one after.

Indossa un elegante   *She is wearing an elegant*
  abito blu.   *blue dress.*

G Adjectives of nationality are spelt with a lower-case initial letter: cinese *Chinese*.

exercise

Add the endings to the adjectives so that they agree in number and gender with the noun.

a Alberto è pazient_____ .   **b** Elena è pover_____ .
c Clelia è una vecchi_____ amica.   **d** Tullio ha un'auto sportiv_____ .   **e** Bill e Jill sono ingles_____ .
f Francesco è generos_____ .   **g** Il caffè italian_____ è aromatic_____ .   **h** Le valige (*suitcases*) sono pesant_____ .

The most common demonstrative adjectives are *questo* (this) and *quello* (that). They need to agree in number and gender with the noun they qualify.

	singular		plural	
	masculine	feminine	masculine	feminine
this/these	**questo** tavolo	**questa** sedia	**questi** tavoli	**queste** sedie
that/those	**quel** libro	**quella** casa	**quei** libri	**quelle** case
	quello zio	**quella** zia	**quegli** zii	**quelle** zie
	quell'amico	**quell'**amica	**quegli** amici	**quelle** amiche

A Questo has the normal feminine and plural forms. The forms of **quello** 'imitate' those of the definite articles.

(il) libro = quel libro *that book*   (i) libri = quei libri *those books*

(lo) zio = quello zio *that uncle*   (gli) zii = quegli zii *those uncles*

(la) zia = quella zia *that aunt*   (le) zie = quelle zie *those aunts*

(l') uomo = quell'uomo *that man*   (gli) uomini = quegli uomini *those men*

(l') asta = quell'asta *that pole*   (le) aste = quelle aste *those poles*

Questo and **quello** take an apostrophe before a vowel.
quest'anno (*this year*); quest'aula (*this classroom*);
quell'anno (*that year*); quell'enciclopedia (*that encyclopedia*).

The plural forms are not shortened except for **quegli** before **i-**:
quegl'italiani *those Italians*

B In the spoken language **questo** (**-a, -i, -e**) can be shortened to **'sto** (**'sta**, etc.) This gave rise to words like **stamattina** (*this morning*), **stasera** (*this evening*) and **stanotte** (*tonight*).

C **Questo** and **quello** can also be pronouns (when they stand instead of a noun: *this/that one, these/those ones*). When used as a pronoun **quello** (and similarly **questo**) takes its usual forms: **quello, quella, quelli** and **quelle**.

Vuole questo o quello?	*Do you want this or that?*
Preferisco quelle.	*I prefer those* (f.pl.) *ones.*

exercise

Complete the sentences below by adding *questo, quest', questa, questi* or *queste*.

a _____ valigia pesa venti chili. (*This suitcase weighs 20 kilos.*)
b _____ scarpe sono troppo strette. (*These shoes are too tight.*)
c _____ ombrello è mio. (*This umbrella is mine.*)
d _____ libri sono pesanti. (*These books are heavy.*)
e _____ casa è un po' piccola. (*This house is a little small.*)
f _____ esercizi sono facili. (*These exercises are easy.*)

Complete the sentences with *quel, quello, quell', quella, quei, quegli* or *quelle*.

g _____ valigia pesa venti chili.
h _____ scarpe sono troppo strette.
i _____ ombrello è mio.
j _____ libri sono pesanti.
k _____ esercizi sono facili.

Indefinite adjectives are those expressing a vague idea of quantity or quality, e.g. *each*, *some*.

A The most common indefinite adjectives are: **ogni** (*each/ every*) and **qualche** (*some/any/a few*). **Qualche** must be followed by a singular noun.

ogni volta	*every time*
ogni giorno	*each day*
Ho qualche libro per te.	*I have some books for you.*
Hai qualche libro per me?	*Have you any books for me?*
Parto tra qualche ora.	*I am leaving in a few hours.*

B *Some* and *a few* are also translated by **alcuni/alcune** followed by a plural masculine or feminine noun, or **di** with the definite article.

Ho alcuni libri per te.	*I have some books for you.*
alcune persone	*some people*
Vorrei delle mele.	*I'd like some apples.*
Ha dei libri sull'ambiente?	*Have you any books on the environment?*

The form with **di** + article is particularly used with unmeasured quantities which are usually referred to in the singular.

Vorrei della stoffa blu. *I'd like some blue material.*

It is not usually used in the negative.

Non ho soldi. *I have no (not any) money.*

C Note the following expressions:
• **qualunque/qualsiasi** (*whatever/whichever/any* in affirmative sentences).

| a qualsiasi costo | *at any cost* |
| Qualsiasi cosa faccia viene criticato. | *Whatever he does he is criticized.* |

- **ciascuno** (*each/every*)

| Ciascuna cartolina costa trenta centesimi. | *Each card costs 30 cents.* |

- **nessuno** (*no/not...any* in negative sentences)

| Non ho nessuna intenzione di andare. | *I have no intention of going.* |

Ciascuno and **nessuno** have a masculine and feminine form. Their ending imitates that of the indefinite articles:
ciascun/nessun libro ciascuno/nessuno studente
ciascun'/nessun'aula (*classroom*)

D **Molto** and **tanto** (*much*), **poco** (*little*), **troppo** (*too much*), **tutto** (*all*), **altro** (*other/another*) always agree in number and gender with the noun they qualify.

| Mangia troppi dolciumi. | *She eats too many cakes.* |
| Ho comprato un'altra penna. | *I bought another pen.* |

exercise

Replace *qualche* with *alcuni/e*. Then read both versions aloud.
E.g. qualche libro → alcuni libri

a Hai qualche rivista? (*Have you some magazines?*)
b Ho atteso qualche ora. (*I waited a few hours.*)
c Andrò tra qualche giorno. (*I am going in a few days.*)
d Ha scritto qualche mese fa. (*S/he wrote some months ago.*)
e Ho comprato qualche regalo. (*I bought a few presents.*)

Possessive adjectives (*my*, etc.) and pronouns (*mine*, etc.) are normally preceded by the article in Italian (*il mio*, etc.).

Masculine		Feminine		
singular	plural	singular	plural	
il mio	i miei	la mia	le mie	*my/mine*
il tuo	i tuoi	la tua	le tue	*your/yours* (informal)
il Suo	i Suoi	la Sua	le Sue	*your/yours* (formal)
il suo	i suoi	la sua	le sue	*his/her/hers*
il nostro	i nostri	la nostra	le nostre	*our/ours*
il vostro	i vostri	la vostra	le vostre	*your/yours* (plural)
il loro	i loro	la loro	le loro	*their/theirs*
il proprio	i propri	la propria	le proprie	*one's*

A Possessive adjectives and pronouns need to agree in gender and number with the noun they qualify rather than with the possessor.

Maria fa il suo lavoro.   *Maria does her job.*

B The article is NOT used before possessive adjectives referring to relations **mia madre** (*my mother*); **mio padre** (*my father*); **mio fratello** (*my brother*); **mia sorella** (*my sister*) – except when the nouns referring to relations are:
- in the plural: le mie sorelle *my sisters*
- followed by an adjective: la mia sorella maggiore *my eldest sister*
- qualified by a suffix, e.g. a diminutive: la mia sorellina *my little sister*

- **mamma** (*mum*), **papà** (*dad*) may – though do not need to – be preceded by the article: (il) mio papà, (la) mia mamma.
- The article is always used before **loro**: il loro figlio *their son*
- After **essere** *mine*, *his*, etc. do not take the article unless some emphasis is required: Questo libro è (il) mio. *This book is mine.*

C Possessive adjectives are used less in Italian than in English, particularly with personal belongings and when accompanied by reflexive verbs.

Ho smarrito il passaporto.	*I have lost my passport.*
Mi lavo le mani.	*I wash my hands.*

Note these constructions: il giornale di oggi *today's newspaper*

Questo non è il mio ombrello, è quello di Maria.	*This is not my umbrella, it is Maria's.*
a casa mia/tua/sua etc.	*at/to my/your/his etc. house.*

exercise

Supply a suitable article when needed.

a Questo è _____ mio ombrello. **b** Quelli sono _____ nostri libri. **c** Queste sono _____ sue cartoline. **d** Questa è _____ loro penna (*pen*). **e** Sono queste _____ tue scarpe (*shoes*)? **f** _____ mio ufficio è in via Roma. **g** _____ vostre scarpe sono pulite (*clean*)? **h** _____ mia madre lavora a Londra.

Interrogative adjectives are used to ask the identity, the quality or the quantity of the noun they qualify.

Che …?	*What …?/Which …?*
Quale(-i) …?	*Which …?*
Quanto(-a, -i, -e) …?	*How much …?/How many …?*

A **Che …?** is invariable.

Che libro è questo?	*What book is this?*
Che macchina hai?	*What car do you have?*

B **Quale …?** is both masculine and feminine. Its plural is **quali**.

Quale libro hai scelto?	*Which book did you choose?*
Quali scarpe preferisci?	*Which shoes do you prefer?*

Before **è** (*is*) and **era** (*was*) **quale** drops its final -e without taking an apostrophe.

Qual è? *Which one is it?*   Qual era? *Which one was it?*

Quale is used to specify a choice between two or more possibilities:

Qual è la tua macchina?	*Which (one) is your car?*
Che macchina hai?	*What car do you have?*

C **Quanto …?** has masculine, feminine and plural forms.

Quanto tè devo comprare?	*How much tea shall I buy?*
Quanta marmellata hai fatto?	*How much jam did you make?*
Quanti voli ci sono al giorno?	*How many flights are there each day?*

| Quante sterline hai? | *How many pounds do you have?* |

D **Che** can also be used in exclamations.

Che peccato!	*What a pity!*
Che noia/Che seccatura!	*What a nuisance!*
Che bell'uomo!	*What a handsome man!*
Che vita!	*What a life!*
Che (bella) sorpresa!	*What a (nice) surprise!*
Che notte!	*What a night!*

exercises

Ask questions choosing the appropriate adjective: *che*, *quale*, *quali*, *quanto*, *quanta*, *quanti*, *quante*.

a _____ tipo di musica preferisci? (*What kind of music do you prefer?*)

b _____ figli ha? (*How many children do you have?*)

c _____ sorelle hai? (*How many sisters do you have?*)

d _____ tempo si ferma? (*How long are you staying?*)

e _____ materia preferisci? (*Which subject do you prefer?*)

f _____ materie studi? (*Which subjects do you study?*)

g _____ libro hai letto? (*Which book did you read?*)

Match these answers to the questions above.

1 Preferisco la musica rock. 2 Soltanto una. 3 Mi fermo due giorni. 4 Studio matematica e informatica. 5 Ho letto 'La tempesta'. 6 Ho tre figli. 7 Preferisco l'informatica.

In English we make comparisons using phrases like *more than* and *as many as*, etc. The same general idea is used in Italian.

più ... di (che)	*more/-er ... than*
meno ... di (che)	*less ... than*
(tanto) ... quanto	*as ... as*
(così) ... come	

A When the comparison is between two things or people (e.g. Anselmo and Giulio) referring to one quality (e.g. **simpatico**), **di** is used.

Anselmo è più simpatico
di Giulio.

*Anselmo is more pleasant
than Giulio.*

Una bici è meno veloce
di una moto.

*A bike is slower than a
motorbike.*

B When the comparison is between two qualities (e.g. **bello** and **simpatico**) referring to one thing or person (e.g. Anselmo), **che** is used.

Anselmo è più bello che
simpatico.

*Anselmo is more handsome
than pleasant.*

C *As ... as ...* is translated by **tanto ... quanto** or **così ... come**. **Tanto** and **così** can be omitted.

Il mio giardino è (così)
bello come il tuo.

Il mio giardino è (tanto)
bello quanto il tuo.

*My garden is as beautiful
as yours.*

D When a comparison concerns a noun, **tanto … quanto** must be used.

Ho tante penne quante te.   *I have as many pens as you.*

(Così) … come is invariable, whereas both parts of (tanto) … quanto need to agree in number and gender with the noun.

exercises

Using the words in the box, write sentences comparing Anselmo with Giulio. Then read the exercise aloud.

E.g. Anselmo è più svelto (*faster*) di Giulio.

---

simpatico (*pleasant*); bello (*handsome*); intelligente (*intelligent*);
studioso (*studious*); ostinato (*obstinate*); mascalzone (*wicked*);
stupido (*stupid*); puntuale (*punctual*); attivo (*active*);
orgoglioso (*proud*); convincente (*convincing*);
prudente (*prudent*); noioso (*boring*)

Re-write the same sentences as above using *meno … di*.

E.g. Giulio è meno svelto di Anselmo.

Carla and Cristina are identical twins. Use the adjectives in the box above to say how identical they are. Remember the adjective has to agree with the gender.

E.g. Carla è (tanto) simpatica quanto Cristina. Carla è (così) bella come Cristina.

In English, *the most* and *the least (of all)* express the highest and lowest levels of a quality. Italian uses a similar structure.

il più ... *the most* ... /*the -est*	il meno ... *the least* ...

A The relative superlative is obtained by placing **il**, **la**, **i** or **le** before **più** or **meno** + adjective.

Concetta è la più studiosa (di tutte).	*Concetta is the most studious (of all).*
Questo libro è il più interessante (di tutti).	*This book is the most interesting (of all).*
L'onestà è la virtù più apprezzata.	*Honesty is the most appreciated virtue.*

When the relative superlative is preceded by a noun, the article goes before that noun and is not repeated immediately before **più** or **meno**.

B The absolute superlative expresses *the most* or *the least* with no comparison. It is formed by dropping the final vowel of the adjective and adding **-issimo**, **-a**, **-i**, **-e**.

bello → bellissimo	*most/very beautiful*

Some adjectives do not take **-issimo**:

- those already expressing an idea of superlative such as colossale (*colossal*), enorme (*enormous*), straordinario (*extraordinary*), etc.

- those having an absolutely precise, specific meaning such as rettangolare (*rectangular*) annuale (*annual*), etc.

C A few adjectives ending in **-re** form the superlative by adding **-errimo**.

| celebre → celeberrimo | *most celebrated* |
| salubre → saluberrimo | *most healthy* |

D The following comparatives and superlatives are irregular.

adjective	comparative	relative superlative	absolute superlative
buono (*good*)	**migliore** (*better*)	**il migliore** (*the best*)	**ottimo** (*very good/excellent*)
cattivo (*bad*)	**peggiore** (*worse*)	**il peggiore** (*the worst*)	**pessimo** (*very bad/terrible*)

exercises

Add *il, la, i, le più/meno* to the sentences below as indicated.

a Oreste è _____ musicista _____ bravo (*most*).
b Angelo è _____ bello dei miei amici (*most*).
c Ho comprato _____ scarpe _____ costose (*least*).
d Annalisa è _____ simpatica di tutte (*most*).

Turn the adjective in each sentence into an absolute superlative. Remember the agreements.

E.g. Questo vestito è caro. ▸ Questo vestito è carissimo.
e Il libro che leggo è interessante. **f** Quell'auto è veloce.
g Mia sorella è intelligente. **h** Mio fratello è studioso.
i Il film era noioso. **j** Teresa è ostinata.

25 irregular adjectives

The adjectives *quello, bello, grande, santo* and *buono* are shortened when used before a noun.

	singular	plural	
m.	quel, quello, quell'	quei, quegli	*that/those*
f.	quella, quell'	quelle	
m.	bel, bello, bell'	bei, begli	*beautiful/nice/*
f.	bella, bell'	belle	*handsome*
m.	gran, grande, grand'	grandi	*large/great*
f.	gran, grande, grand'	grandi	
m.	san, santo, sant'	santi	*saint*
f.	santa, sant'	sante	
m.	buon, buono	buoni	*good*
f.	buona, buon'	buone	

A Quello and bello imitate the definite article (il, lo, la, l', i, gli, le):

quel libro (*that book*), quei libri (*those books*)
quello studente (*that student*), quegli studenti (*those students*)
bell'uomo (*handsome man*), begli uomini (*handsome men*)
bella casa (*beautiful house*), belle case (*beautiful houses*)

B Grande and santo usually become gran and san before masculine singular nouns starting with a consonant except for z- and s- followed by consonant. Gran is occasionally used before feminine nouns starting with a consonant.

un grande santo (*a great saint*); un grand'uomo (*a great man*); un gran successo (*a great success*); una grande casa (*a large house*); un gran cosa (*a great thing*).

San Gerolamo, Sant'Angelo, Santo Stefano, Sant'Agnese, Santa Teresa

una grand'idea (*a great idea*); due grandi libri (*two great books*); due grandi case (*two large houses*)

C Buono imitates the indefinite article **un/uno/una/un'**.
un buon libro (*a good book*); un buono studente (*a good student*); una buona commedia (*a good play*); una buon'idea (*a good idea*)

exercises

Fill in the appropriate form of *quell', quel, quello, quella, quegli,* etc.

a _____ uomo è un genio.

b _____ ragazza viene da Lucca.

c _____ aereo ha 360 posti.

d _____ studenti sono veramente bravi.

e Non ho letto _____ libro.

f Mi piace _____ specchio.

g _____ riviste costano care.

h _____ film è eccellente.

Enter the right form of *grande*.

E.g. Einstein era un _____ uomo. → Einstein era un grand'uomo.

i un _____ seccatore (*bore*)

j una _____ battaglia (*battle*)

k Le Alpi sono _____ montagne.

l una _____ esperienza

m due _____ errori

n È un _____ peccato (*great pity*).

Cardinal numbers (one, two, three, etc.) are adjectives expressing a definite quantity.

1 uno	16 sedici	100 cento
2 due	17 diciassette	101 centouno
3 tre	18 diciotto	102 centodue
4 quattro	19 diciannove	103 centotré
5 cinque	20 venti	200 duecento
6 sei	21 ventuno	300 trecento
7 sette	22 ventidue	1.000 mille
8 otto	23 ventitré	2.000 duemila
9 nove	30 trenta	10.000 diecimila
10 dieci	40 quaranta	100.000 centomila
11 undici	50 cinquanta	1.000.000 un milione
12 dodici	60 sessanta	10.000.000 dieci milioni
13 tredici	70 settanta	100.000.000 cento milioni
14 quattordici	80 ottanta	1.000.000.000 un miliardo
15 quindici	90 novanta	1.000.000.000.000 un bilione

A Numbers are invariable except for **zero** (*zero, nought* and 0 for telephone numbers), which has a plural form (**zeri**), **uno** which follows the same rule as the indefinite article (**un, uno, una, un'**), **mille**, the plural of which is **mila**, and the nouns **milione, miliardo** and **bilione**.

B **Venti, trenta,** etc. drop the final vowel when followed by **uno** or **otto: trentuno, trentotto, quarantuno, quarantotto.**

Ventuno, trentuno, etc. drop their final **-o** before a noun.
  quarantun anni *41 years*

Tre combined with **venti, trenta, quaranta**, etc. acquires an acute accent on the -e: quattrocentoventitré

CNumbers are normally written as one word (**millenove-centonovantanove**). **Milione, miliardo** and **bilione** are written separately: un milione (*one million*)

Thousands are separated by a dot rather than a comma as in English, and Italian uses a comma for the decimal point:
£ 375,726 = 375.726 sterline
1.52 *one point five two* = 1,52 uno virgola cinquantadue

In day-to-day transactions **e** (*and*) is said instead of **virgola**.
Un euro e ventisette (centesimi)   *One euro and 27.*

exercises

Write the numbers below out in full, then read them aloud.
5 6 7 11 12 13 14 15 16 17 19 20 27 28 30 36 38
140 167 1.576 1.769   2.006 16.596 26.700 137.766
10.758.756   5,8 1,6 3,7 15,9 28,6 74,5 115,9 3.456,98

Read aloud these sentences then re-write them with the prices in numerals.
a I pomodori costano due (euro) e ventisette (centesimi).
b Queste mele costano due euro al chilo.
c In tutto spende quattro (euro) e trentanove (centesimi).
d Queste banane costano uno e cinquantacinque.
e Le pere costano due e settantotto.
f Le fragole costano tre e quarantuno al cestino (*punnet*).

Ordinal numbers (1st, 2nd, 3rd, etc.) indicate a position in an order or a series. They agree in gender and number with the noun.

1st primo	5th quinto	9th nono	100th centesimo
2nd secondo	6th sesto	10th decimo	1,000th millesimo
3rd terzo	7th settimo	11th undicesimo	2,000th duemillesimo
4th quarto	8th ottavo	12th dodicesimo	10,000th diecimillesimo

A Ordinal numbers from 11th onwards are formed from the cardinal number minus the final vowel + **-esimo**, except for 23rd, 33rd, 43rd, etc. which keep the vowel:
  ventitreesimo, trentatreesimo, quarantatreesimo

Duemila, tremila, etc. become **duemillesimo, tremillesimo,** etc.

B Ordinal numbers agree in gender and number with the noun they precede: le prime parole (*the first words*);
  il decimo capitolo (*the 10th chapter*);
  la quinta sinfonia di Beethoven (*Beethoven's fifth symphony*).

C Ordinal numbers can be written in Roman (II, XI) or as cardinal numbers followed by ° for the masculine and ª for the feminine: $2° = 2nd$ (m), $10ª = 10th$ (f)

With monarchs and popes they are usually written in Roman characters and follow the noun but, unlike English, the article is not said:
  Enrico VIII (Enrico Ottavo) *Henry VIII*

D Some Italian streets are named after historical dates using Roman but read as cardinal numbers, e.g. Via XX Settembre (Via Venti Settembre). Below is a list of Roman numerals with their Arabic equivalents.

1 I	11 XI	21 XXI	40 XL	500 D
2 II	12 XII	22 XXII	50 L	600 DC
3 III	13 XIII	23 XXIII	60 LX	700 DCC
4 IV	14 XIV	24 XXIV	70 LXX	800 DCCC
5 V	15 XV	25 XXV	80 LXXX	900 CM
6 VI	16 XVI	26 XXVI	90 XC	1000 M
7 VII	17 XVII	27 XXVII	100 C	2000 MM
8 VIII	18 XVIII	28 XXVIII	200 CC	
9 IX	19 XIX	29 XXIX	300 CCC	
10 X	20 XX	30 XXX	400 CD	

exercise

Translate the following. Remember the agreements.

a the 11th chapter (**capitolo**)

b the ninth symphony by Beethoven

c the third man (**uomo**)

d the 17th century

e the 2nd on the right
(**a destra**)

f the fourth daughter (**figlia**)

g the second son (**figlio**)

h the third leg (**tappa**)

i first gear (**marcia**)

j Fifth Avenue (**strada**)

k the 3rd on the left
(**a sinistra**)

l the tenth Commandment
(**Comandamento**)

The Italian way of naming centuries is slightly different to the English.

A Ordinal numbers are used to name centuries (**secoli**) and are often written in Roman numerals, in which case they usually follow the noun.

il secolo XX/il 20° secolo

B From the 13th century to the 20th century there are alternative expressions equivalent to saying *the twelve hundreds*, etc. in English; centuries are represented by cardinal numbers used as nouns; **mille** is omitted; and when written in letters the intial letter is capital.

(year 1201–1300)	il Duecento	il secolo XIII	(13°)
(year 1301–1400)	il Trecento	il secolo XIV	(14°)
(year 1401–1500)	il Quattrocento	il secolo XV	(15°)
(year 1501–1600)	il Cinquecento	il secolo XVI	(16°)
(year 1601–1700)	il Seicento	il secolo XVII	(17°)
(year 1701–1800)	il Settecento	il secolo XVIII	(18°)
(year 1801–1900)	l'Ottocento	il secolo XIX	(19°)
(year 1901–2000)	il Novecento	il secolo XX	(20°)

In English we refer to years as being BC (before Christ) and AD (Anno Domini). In Italian, BC becomes **a.C.** (**avanti Cristo**) and AD becomes **d.C.** (**dopo Cristo**).

Dal X al III secolo a.C.
i popoli italici parlavano
etrusco.

*From the tenth to the
third century BC the Italic
peoples spoke Etruscan.*

| Giacomo Leopardi è un grande poeta dell'Ottocento. | *Giacomo Leopardi is a great poet of the 1800s.* |

In popular use centuries are calculated, for example, from 1st January 1800 to 31st December 1899.

C *Millennium* is translated by **millennio**.

| Il primo millennio è terminato il 31 dicembre 999, il secondo va dal 1° gennaio 1000 al 31 dicembre 1999. | *The first millennium ended on the 31st December 999, the second goes from the 1st January 1000 to the 31st December 1999.* |

In Italian years are written as one word: **duemilatré**.

In popular use the millennium is calculated, for example, from 1 January 2000 to 31 December 2999.

exercise

True or false?

a Leonardo da Vinci nacque (*was born*) nel 1452: nel Quattrocento.

b Cristoforo Colombo scoprì (*discovered*) l'America nel 1492: nel XV secolo.

c Guglielmo Marconi inventò (*invented*) la radio nel 1901: nel Novecento.

d Galileo Galilei nacque (*was born*) nel 1564: nel 16° secolo.

e L'Italia fu unita (*was united*) nel 1862: nell'800 d.C.

f Nel 79 d.C. l'eruzione del Vesuvio distrusse (*destroyed*) Pompei: nel I° secolo.

g Nel 1778 Alessandro Volta inventò la batteria elettrica: nell'Ottocento.

Fractions are made as in English by saying the cardinal followed by the ordinal number. *Un* before *mezzo* is usually omitted.

A ½ ((un) mezzo) ⅗ (tre quinti) ⅞ (sette ottavi) ⁹⁄₁₀ (nove decimi)

Mezzo (*half*) agrees with the nouns it refers to: mezzo chilo di pane (*half a kilo of bread*); mezza bottiglia di vino (*half a bottle of wine*)

B Mathematical signs

+ più	: *or* ÷ diviso
− meno	= uguale a/fa/fanno
× per/moltiplicato	% percento

C Multiple numbers: doppio (*double*); triplo (*treble*); quadruplo (*quadruple*)

D Iterative numbers: una volta (*once*); due volte (*twice*); tre volte (*three times*)

E Collective numbers: **un paio** (*a pair*) generally refers to things: **una coppia** (*a couple*) generally refers to people or animals.

un paio di panini (*a couple of rolls*); una coppia di sposi (*a married couple*); una coppia di cavalli (*a pair of horses*)

Note also the following:
una/mezza dozzina (*a/half a dozen*); una decina (*about ten*); una ventina (*about twenty*); un migliaio (*about a thousand*); un centinaio (*about a hundred*)

una dozzina di uova *a dozen eggs*
C'era una ventina di persone. *There were about twenty people.*

F Other expressions to indicate how people or things are divided:
- **ad uno ad uno** (*one by one*), **a due a due/due per due** (*two by two*) etc.
- **uno/due/tre alla volta** (*one/two/three at a time*)
- **ambedue** (invariable), **tutti e due** (feminine form = **tutte e due**) and **entrambi** (feminine form = **entrambe**), mean *both*.

Entrambe le ragazze sono cinesi. *Both girls are Chinese.*
Ambedue i coniugi sono italiani. *Both spouses are Italian.*

G Nouns indicating a period of time: biennio (*two years*); triennio (*three years*); quadriennio (*four years*); decennio (*ten years*); ventennio (*twenty years*); bimestre (*two months*); trimestre (*three months*); quadrimestre (*four months*); semestre (*six months*)

Other words and expressions: **gemelli** (*twins*); **bambino trigemino** (*triplet*); **la triplice Alleanza** (*the Triple Alliance*)

exercise

Write *mezzo*, *mezza* or *mezz'* as appropriate in the spaces.

a _____ litro di latte		**e** _____ chilometro	
b _____ pinta di birra		**f** _____ ora	
c _____ bottiglia d'acqua		**g** _____ biglietto (*ticket*)	
d _____ chilo di spaghetti		**h** _____ dozzina di uova	

The days of the week, months, dates and seasons.

A The days of the week are written with a small initial letter. Note that they are all masculine except for **domenica**. No word is used to say *on* a day. The definite article **il/la** is used to indicate recurrence:

la domenica   *on Sundays*

I GIORNI DELLA SETTIMANA *(the days of the week)*			
lunedì	*Monday*	venerdì	*Friday*
martedì	*Tuesday*	sabato	*Saturday*
mercoledì	*Wednesday*	domenica	*Sunday*
giovedì	*Thursday*		

Che giorno è oggi?	*What day (of the week) is*
Oggi è lunedì.	*it today? Today is Monday.*
Ci vediamo martedì.	*See you on Tuesday.*
Ci vediamo martedì prossimo.	*See you next Tuesday.*
Il martedì vado all'università.	*On Tuesdays I go to the university.*
martedì mattina/pomeriggio/sera/ notte/scorso/prossimo	*Tuesday morning/afternoon/ evening/night/last/next*

B Months are also written with a small initial letter.

gennaio	*January*	maggio	*May*	settembre	*September*
febbraio	*February*	giugno	*June*	ottobre	*October*
marzo	*March*	luglio	*July*	novembre	*November*
aprile	*April*	agosto	*August*	dicembre	*December*

Quanti ne abbiamo oggi?	*What day is it today?*
Ne abbiamo tre.	*It's the third.*
Che data è oggi?	*What's the date today?*
È il due luglio.	*It's the second of July.*

C The days of the month are written (and spoken) in cardinal numbers except for the first: il primo maggio, il due, il tre etc. *the first of May, the 2nd, the 3rd etc.*

D Seasons: la primavera (*spring*); l'estate (f.) (*summer*); l'autunno (*autumn*); l'inverno (*winter*)

In can be translated by either **in** or **di**. **Primavera** can also take **a**.

in/di/a primavera *in spring*	in/d'estate *in summer*
in/d'autunno *in autumn*	in/d'inverno *in winter*

exercise

Translate the following into Italian.

a See you on Monday.
b I will see you next week.
c Every Tuesday I go to the cinema.
d On Wednesdays I go to my Italian lesson.
e I go to the disco on Sundays.
f On Monday afternoons I go to the gym.
g On Saturday mornings I go riding (**vado a cavalcare**).
h On Friday evenings I go to the theatre.
i What day (of the week) is it? It's Thursday.
j What is the date today? It's the first of June.

The verb is the most important (and most variable) part of speech. It indicates the action or the state of a person, animal or thing.

A Verbs have different moods which convey the manner in which the action is carried out, since it is important to know whether the action is really happening, or if it depends on a condition, or if it is only probable.

B It is also necessary to know the tense. This indicates the time at which the speaker places the action expressed by the verb (present, past, future). The tense can be simple or compound, the latter being formed by an auxiliary verb (so called because it 'assists' the main verb – usually *to be* or *to have*) followed by the verb expressing the action.

C Equally important is the subject (*I*, *you*, etc.) which tells you who is doing or undergoing the action expressed by the verb. Italian subject pronouns are seldom used because – with a few exceptions – each of the verbs has a different ending, each one conveying which person it refers to.

D The infinitive of a verb, which in English is preceded by *to*, e.g. *to speak*, *to see*, *to leave*, is expressed in Italian by one of three types of ending. They are: -**are** (called verbs of the first type or first conjugation); -**ere** (verbs of the second type or second conjugation); -**ire** (verbs of the third type or third conjugation).

Parlare, vedere, partire are infinitives. The first part (parl-, ved-, part-) is known as the 'root' or 'stem'. The second part (-are, -ere, -ire) is the ending or suffix.

E To form the right tense and person of a verb involves changing the -are, -ere or -ire ending and applying another to the stem. For instance, **parl-** has an -o added to make **parlo** (*I speak*) or -avo added to make **parlavo** (*I was speaking*).

F Most Italian tenses follow a fixed pattern but several do not (like *to be* in English). These irregular verbs will have to be learned separately. They mostly belong to the second type (-ere). You will also come across some irregular infinitives ending in -urre, -arre and -orre like **produrre** (*to produce*), **tradurre** (*to translate*), **proporre** (*to propose*) and **estrarre** (*to extract*): these belong to the -ere type, since they come from the old forms **producere, traducere, proponere** and **estraere**.

exercise

Sort the verbs below into three categories according to their endings (-*are*, -*ere*, -*ire*). Then change the ending into -*o* to give the first person singular *io* (*I*) form. *E.g.* *mangiare → (io) mangio.*

a dormire (*to sleep*) **b** camminare (*to walk*) **c** partire (*to depart*) **d** parlare (*to speak*) **e** guardare (*to look (at)*) **f** vedere (*to see*) **g** comprare (*to buy*) **h** ascoltare (*to listen to*) **i** volare (*to fly*) **j** ridere (*to laugh*) **k** prendere (*to take*) **l** mettere (*to put*) **m** vivere (*to live*) **n** piangere (*to cry*) **o** ballare (*to dance*)

Infinitives have three types of endings: *-are, -ere* and *-ire*. To form the present tense, change the infinitive ending.

	PARLARE *to speak*	VEDERE *to see*	PARTIRE *to leave*
(io) *I* (tu) *you* (*informal*) (lui/lei/Lei) (*he/she/it*; *you* (*formal*)	parl-**o** parl-**i** parl-**a**	ved-**o** ved-**i** ved-**e**	part-**o** part-**i** part-**e**
(noi) *we* (voi) *you* (*pl. informal*) (loro/Loro) *they*; *you* (*pl. formal*)	parl-**iamo** parl-**ate** parl-**ano**	ved-**iamo** ved-**ete** ved-**ono**	part-**iamo** part-**ite** part-**ono**

Parla italiano, signora?	*Do you speak Italian, madam?*
Parto.	*I am leaving.*
Vedono il film adesso.	*They are watching the film now.*
Partiamo domani.	*We leave tomorrow.*

Remember that the subject pronoun is rarely used.

A When using the formal *you*, the third person singular must be used.

    Parla italiano, signore?   *Do you speak Italian, sir?*

B The plural form of the formal *you* uses the third person plural, although the second person plural can be safely used:

    Parlano italiano, signori? }
    Parlate italiano?   *Do you speak Italian, gentlemen?*

C Verbs ending in **-iare** do not need the addition of an **-i** in the

second person singular and the first plural: tu mangi *you eat*
noi mangiamo *we eat*

D Pronunciation. The stress always goes on the stem except for
the first and second person plural

parlo, parli, parla, parliamo, parlate, parlano

E The present tense is also used to express:
• continuous action: Adesso mangio. *I am eating now.*

• the future
Domani parto.   *I leave/I am leaving/I am going to leave tomorrow.*

• an action started in the past but still continuing
Abito in Inghilterra da 25 anni. *I have been living in England
for 25 years.*

exercise

Translate the following into Italian.

a You (*pl. informal*) see?
b I do not speak German (**tedesco**).
c They always (**sempre**) speak of you (*formal*).
d She speaks all the time (**sempre**).
e Do you speak English (**inglese**)?
f I see my mother every day.
g Can you see my glasses (**occhiali**)?
h I have been living here for a year.
i Are you (*informal*) leaving today (**oggi**)?

There are some verbs that, although regular in their endings, have stems which behave differently.

A Some verbs of the third type (those ending in **-ire**) have an **-isc** placed between the stem and the ending, except for the first and second persons plural.

FINIRE *to finish*	
fin-**isc**-o	I finish
fin-**isc**-i	you (sing. informal) finish
fin-**isc**-e	he/she/it finishes, you (sing. formal) finish
fin-**iamo**	we finish
fin-**ite**	you finish
fin-**isc**-ono	they/you (plural formal) finish

Among the commonest verbs belonging to this group are: agire (*to act*); capire (*to understand*); condire (*to season*); costruire (*to build*); guarire (*to heal*); preferire (*to prefer*); proibire (*to forbid*); pulire (*to clean*); restituire (*to give back*); sparire (*to disappear*); spedire (*to send*)

Pay attention when pronouncing these verbs since **-isc** followed by a consonant is pronounced **isk**, but if followed by **-i** or **-e** is pronounced **ish**.

B Some verbs like **cercare** (*to look for, to search*) and **pagare** (*to pay*), in order to preserve the hard sound of the **-c** or the

-g, add an **-h** before the **-i** or the **-e** of the ending:
    cercare   cerco, cerchi, cerca, cerchiamo, cercate, cercano
    pagare   pago, paghi, paga, paghiamo, pagate, pagano

C Other verbs, like **salire** (*to go up/to get on a bus*, etc.),
spegnere (*to switch off*), **tenere** (*to keep/to hold*), **rimanere**
(*to stay/to remain*) and **scegliere** (*to choose*), have their own
irregularities.

salire	salgo, sali, sale, saliamo, salite, salgono
spegnere	spengo, spegni, spegne, spegniamo, spegnete, spengono
tenere	tengo, tieni, tiene, teniamo, tenete, tengono
rimanere	rimango, rimani, rimane, rimaniamo, rimanete, rimangono
scegliere	scelgo, scegli, sceglie, scegliamo, scegliete, scelgono

exercise

Change the sentences below into the plural form.

E.g. Giorgio finisce di lavorare alle sei → Giorgio e
Giovanni finiscono di lavorare alle sei.

a Io finisco di lavorare all'una. Noi ...
b Luisa capisce il russo. Luisa e Giacomo ...
c Tu preferisci rimanere a casa? Voi ...
d Enrico agisce con prudenza. Enrico ed Antonio ...
e Mario costruisce una casa. Mario e Giorgio ...
f Carla pulisce la casa. Carla e Lia ...

34 subject pronouns

Personal pronouns, which include subject pronouns, are used instead of nouns. *I, you, he,* **etc. are subject pronouns.**

singular		plural	
io	*I*	noi	*we*
tu	*you (sing. informal)*	voi	*you (pl. informal)*
lui (egli); esso	*he; it (m.)*	loro (essi/esse)	*they*
lei (ella); essa	*she; it (f.)*	Loro	*you (pl. formal)*
Lei	*you (sing. formal)*		

A When used, the subject pronoun normally precedes the verb but, unlike English, it is usually omitted.

   Vado.   *I am going.*

Subject pronouns are used:
• for emphasis

   Io vado.   *I am going.*

   For even greater emphasis, it can be placed after the verb.

   Vado io!   *I am going (not you/you needn't).*

• with **Lei** (the formal you) as a form of courtesy when addressing a person

   Lei è inglese?   *Are you English (sir/madam)?*

• when the action, opinion, etc. of one person differs from that of another

   Io sono inglese, lui è francese. *I am English, he is French.*

B **Tu** is used with close friends, children and members of one's family.

C Egli, ella, essi and esse are mainly confined to formal written language. **Lui, lei** and **loro** are used instead. **Esso** and **essa** can also be used for animals, though they are usually avoided since they sound old fashioned and affected.

D Lei (the formal *you*) is often written with a capital letter and used to address adults who are not close friends. It is followed by the third person singular form of the verb.

Lei è inglese, signora?   *Are you English, madam?*

You here is something like *your excellency.*

The subject pronoun can go at the end of a question.
È inglese Lei?

The formal plural **Loro** is also written with the capital letter.
Loro sono tutti inglesi?   *Are you all English?* (lit.: *Are they all English?*)

The rule on its use is more flexible: **voi** can be used without giving offence:
Voi siete tutti inglesi?   *Are you all English?*

exercise

In which of these sentences would you not use the subject pronoun? Delete it when you think it is not needed.

a Io sono inglese. (*I am English.*)
b Io sono inglese e Lei? (*I am English, and you?*)
c Io esco, ti serve qualcosa? (*I am going out, do you need something?*)
d Io esco e tu? (*I am going out, and you?*)

As their name suggests, *me, him, her*, etc. do not stand for
the subject but for the object, that is, for the 'receiver' of the
action of the verb.

singular		plural	
mi	*me*	ci	*us*
ti	*you (sing.)*	vi	*you (pl.)*
lo	*him; it (m.)*	li	*them (m.)*
la	*her; it (f.)*	le	*them (f.)*
La	*you (formal)*		

A Unlike English, the direct object pronoun precedes the verb.
Mi vedi? *Do you see me?* Lo vedo. *I see him.*
La vedo. *I see her.*

B The singular formal form of *you* is **La**, the same as *her*,
written with a capital 'L'.

La trovo molto bene,	*I find you very well,*
signor Rossi.	*Mr Rossi.*

The plural formal masculine and feminine forms are
respectively **Li** and **Le**: Li trovo molto bene, signori. Le trovo
molto bene, signore.

If the persons addressed are of mixed gender, the masculine
form is used.

C Direct object pronouns are added to the end of infinitives,
gerunds, past participles and some imperatives. Note the loss
of the verb's final vowel.

Posso presentarLe Maria? *May I introduce you to Maria?*

Prendilo con te.   *Take it with you.*

D **Lo** and **la** take an apostrophe before a vowel or **h-**: L'amo.
I love it/him/her. L'ho. *I have it.* **Mi, ti, ci** and **vi** are treated
similarly, although the full form is more common: M'aiuta
nei lavori domestici. *He/She helps me with the housework.*

E Past participles must agree with **lo, la, li** and **le**.
Ho preso il caffè. L'ho preso.   *I had the coffee. I had it.*
Ho preso l'auto. L'ho presa.   *I got the car. I got it.*
Ho preso i biglietti. Li ho presi. *I got the tickets. I got them.*
Ho preso le pillole. Le ho prese. *I took the pills. I took them.*

When the object is at the beginning of the sentence, **lo, la, li**
and **le** follow it, giving the sentence two objects.
Le chiavi le hai?   *Do you have the keys?* (lit. *The*
                                   keys do you have them?)

cxercise
**Re-write the statements or answer the questions using the
direct object pronoun instead of the noun when needed.**

E.g. Vedo Giovanni. → Lo vedo. Prendi le pillole? → Sì, ... Le
prendo.

a Vedi quella nave? Sì, ...   f Prendi la medicina? Sì, ...
b Vedete i miei occhiali? Sì,   g Prendi i biglietti? Sì, ...
c La domenica vedo i miei amici. h T'aiuta Marco? Sì, ...
d Ci vedete? Sì, ...   i Vediamo i film alla TV.
e Prendo l'autobus (m.).   j I vostri figli vi aiutano? Sì, ...

The indirect object pronoun 'receives' the action carried out by the subject: *She gave him a present.* = *She gave a present to him.*

stressed		unstressed
a me	*to me*	mi
a te	*to you*	ti
a lui	*to him*	gli
a lei	*to her*	le
a Lei	*to you (formal)*	Le
a noi	*to us*	ci
a voi	*to you (pl.)*	vi
a loro	*to them*	loro/gli
a Loro	*to you (formal pl.)*	Loro/gli

A The stressed form gives emphasis to the pronoun which, as in English, goes at the end of the sentence.

Maria ha fatto un regalo a lui. *Maria gave a present to him.*

B The more common unstressed form follows the same rules as the direct object pronoun except for **loro**, which is placed after the verb.

| Le do il libro. | *I give her the book.* |
| Do loro il libro. | *I give them the book.* |

Nevertheless, nowadays **gli** can be used instead of the more pedantic **loro**, the latter being confined to written or literary use, so **Gli do il libro** can mean either *I give him the book* or *I give them the book*.

C With the exception of **loro**, indirect object pronouns are added to the end of infinitives (after the loss of the final vowel), gerunds, past participles and some imperatives.

Voglio parlargli.   *I want to speak to him.*

D As well as *to me, to him, to her*, etc., the indirect pronoun can, in some cases, translate *for me, for him*, etc. or even *of him, of her*, etc.

Gli ho fatto una foto.   *I took a picture of him.*
Le ho comprato un profumo.   *I bought (for) her some perfume.*

English expressions like *I rang him, I told her*, etc. mean *I rang to him, I said to her* and are therefore translated **Gli ho telefonato, Le ho detto.**

exercise
Translate the following twice, using first the stressed form, then the unstressed form.

E.g. **Eva ha fatto un regalo a lui. Eva gli ha fatto un regalo.**
a Eva gave a present to me.   b Eva gave a present to you (*inform. sing.*).   c Eva gave a present to him.   d Eva gave a present to her.   e Eva gave a present to us.   f Eva gave a present to you (*inform. pl.*).   g Eva gave a present to them.

Translate the following into Italian.
h I give her a book.   i I give him a book.   j I took a picture of them.   k I bought them a chandelier (**lampadario**).   l They bought me a suitcase.   m I told her the truth (**la verità**).

When indirect and direct object pronouns occur in the same sentence, they come together and precede the verb (except in the case of *loro* which follows the verb).

INDIRECT OBJECT PRONOUNS + DIRECT OBJECT PRONOUNS = COMBINED PRONOUNS				
	+ lo	+ la	+ li	+ le
mi	me lo [*verb*]	me la [*verb*]	me li [*verb*]	me le [*verb*]
ti	te lo [*verb*]	te la [*verb*]	te li [*verb*]	te le [*verb*]
gli, le, Le	glielo [*verb*]	gliela [*verb*]	glieli [*verb*]	gliele [*verb*]
ci	ce lo [*verb*]	ce la [*verb*]	ce li [*verb*]	ce le [*verb*]
vi	ve lo [*verb*]	ve la [*verb*]	ve li [*verb*]	ve le [*verb*]
gli	glielo [*verb*]	gliela [*verb*]	glieli [*verb*]	gliele [*verb*]
loro	lo [*verb*] loro	la [*verb*] loro	li [*verb*] loro	le [*verb*] loro

A Mi, ti, ci, etc. become **me, te, ce,** etc. **Gli** and **le** etc. combine to become **glie** which is applicable to the masculine, feminine and formal *you* forms.

Ci dai la cassetta?	*Will you give us the cassette?*
Ve la darò domani.	*I will give it to you tomorrow.*
Me la vendi?	*Will you sell it* (feminine) *to me?*
Gli hai dato i libri?	*Did you give him the books?*
Glieli ho dati ieri.	*I gave them to him yesterday.*

B If the third person plural **loro** is used instead of **gli**, it must follow the verb.

Glielo dirò domani. ⎫
Lo dirò loro domani. ⎭   *I will tell them tomorrow.*

C The partitive **ne** (*some/of it/of them/about it/about them*) combines in the same way as **lo, la, li, le.**

Me ne manderà una dozzina.   *She'll send me a dozen of them.*
Gliene parlerò domani.   *I will speak to him about it tomorrow.*

Note that often in English *of it/of them* is not used.

Quanti anni hai? Ne ho venti. *How old are you? I am twenty.* (lit. *How many years have you? I have twenty of them.*)

D With the verbs **potere** (*to be able/may/can*), **dovere** (*must/to have to*) and **volere** (*to want*) + an infinitive, direct, indirect or combined pronouns can either precede the verb or be attached to the following infinitive.

Lo voglio vedere./Voglio vederlo. *I want to see him.*
Gli devo parlare./Devo parlargli. *I must talk to him.*

exercise

Answer these questions using the appropriate combined pronouns.

E.g. **Mi dai la chiave?** → **Te la darò (domani).**

a Mi dai il libro?
b Gli dai la cassetta?
c Le dai il disco?
d Ci dai mille euro?
e Le dai un po' di torta?
f Ci dai le video-cassette?

The use of pronouns preceded by a preposition (*with*, *for*, etc.) and the use of *ci* and *vi*.

PRONOUNS PRECEDED BY A PREPOSITION OTHER THAN **a**		
singular		plural
me	*me*	noi *us*
te	*you*	voi *you* (pl.)
lui	*him*	essi
lei	*her*	esse } *them*
Lei	*you* (formal)	loro
esso/a (masc./fem.)	*it*	

A These pronouns are used after prepositions (apart from **a**). **Esso, essa, essi** and **esse** refer mainly to objects but are seldom used.

B As can be seen from the above list, these pronouns are very similar to subject pronouns (see Unit 34) except for the first two persons singular.

C'è posta per me?	*Is there any mail for me?*
Vado da lui.	*I am going to him.*
Mi ricordo di lei.	*I remember her.*
Chi viene con Lei, signora?	*Who is coming with you, madam?*
Mario viene con noi.	*Mario is coming with us.*

C Uses of **ci** and **vi**.
Apart from *us/to us,* **ci** can also be an adverb meaning *here* or *there*.

C'è/Non c'è	*There is/There is not*
Ci sono/Non ci sono	*There are/There are not*
Ci vado ogni giorno.	*I go there every day.*
Ci vengo ogni giorno.	*I come here every day.*
Ci sono dodici mesi in un anno.	*There are twelve months in a year.*
C'è un bar qui vicino?	*Is there a bar near here?*

Additionally it can mean *in it/about it/about them.*

| Non ci credo. | *I don't believe in it.* |
| Ci penso sempre. | *I always think about it/ him/her/them.* |

Vi in this context is identical to **ci** but is more used in writing.

exercise

Re-organize the words to make meaningful sentences.

a ricordo mi lui di
b lui da vado
c viene lei con chi (*whom*)?
d Marianna noi con viene
e una c'è per lettera voi
f ricordo di mi lui non

g ricordo non mi lei di
h con viene Gisella noi?
i messaggio c'è per un te
j lei di ricordo mi
k pacco è questo te per
l giornali per lui sono questi

The English verb *to be* doesn't follow the regular pattern: it is irregular. It is also irregular in Italian, as are several other verbs.

ESSERE *to be*			
(io)	sono	inglese/inglesi	(*English*)
		di Londra	(*from London*)
(tu)	sei	in banca	(*in the bank*)
		in aereo	(*on a plane*)
(lui)/Paolo		in Europa	(*in Europe*)
(lei)/Marianna		in ufficio	(*in the office*)
(Lei)	è	in treno	(*on a train*)
La signora Simoni		in autobus	(*on the bus*)
Il signor Simoni		in barca	(*on the boat*)
		in discoteca	(*at the disco*)
(noi)	siamo	al cinema	(*at the cinema*)
		a teatro	(*at the theatre*)
(voi)	siete	alla mensa	(*in the canteen*)
		alla posta	(*at the post office*)
(loro)		alla partita	(*at the match*)
(Loro)		a Capri	(*in Capri*)
I ragazzi	sono	a Milano	(*in Milan*)
Le ragazze		a scuola	(*at school*)
		a casa	(*at home*)

Siamo a Capri.	*We are in Capri.*
La signora è a casa.	*The lady is at home.*
Chi sono?	*Who are they?*
Sono Paolo e Marianna.	*It is* (lit.:*They are*) *Paolo and Marianna.*
Io sono inglese.	*I am English.*
Loro non sono italiani.	*They are not Italian.*
C'è una banca in questa via?	*Is there a bank in this street?*
Dov'è Paolo?	*Where is Paolo?*
Dove sono Paolo e Maria?	*Where are Paolo and Maria?*

exercise

Fill the spaces in this conversation with the correct form of the verb.

— Scusi, 1 dov'_____ la segreteria?
— Al secondo piano (*floor*).
— Che cosa 2 _____ necessario fare per iscriversi (*enrol*) a questo corso?
— 3 _____ necessario 4 _____ (*to pay*) la tassa d'iscrizione, avere due foto, il passaporto e il suo indirizzo in Italia.
— Quante ore di lezione ci 5 _____ in questo corso?
— Ci 6 _____ trenta ore la settimana.
— 7 _____ _____ lezioni il sabato?
— Il sabato 8 _____ _____ gite ed escursioni.
— E la domenica?
— La domenica 9 _____ _____ uno spettacolo teatrale.

The verb *avere* (to have) is another irregular verb.

AVERE *to have*			
(io)	ho	una macchina nuova	(*a new car*)
		moltissimi amici	(*loads of friends*)
(tu)	hai	un libro da scrivere	(*a book to write*)
		una casa in campagna	(*a house in the country*)
(lui)/Paolo		una barca a motore	(*a motorboat*)
(lei)/Marianna		l'influenza	(*the flu*)
(Lei)	ha	molti soldi	(*a lot of money*)
La signora Simoni		gli occhi azzurri	(*blue eyes*)
Il signor Simoni		una carta di credito	(*a credit card*)
		due biglietti gratis	(*two free tickets*)
(noi)	abbiamo	molti vestiti	(*many clothes*)
		un giardino enorme	(*a large garden*)
(voi)	avete	(il) mal di testa	(*a headache*)
(loro)		moltissimi libri	(*very many books*)
(Loro)		due figli	(*two sons/children*)
I ragazzi	hanno	uno chalet al mare	(*a chalet by the sea*)
Le ragazze		i capelli biondi	(*blond hair*)

Ha una carta di credito, signora?	*Do you have a credit card, madam?*
Il signor Simoni ha due figli.	*Mr Simoni has two children.*
Chi ha il mio passaporto?	*Who has my passport?*

Dove hai messo il mio libro?	*Where have you put my book?*
Non ho molti soldi.	*I don't have a lot of money.*
Paolo ha gli occhi azzurri.	*Paul has blue eyes.*
Che barca hanno, Loro?	*What boat do you* (formal) *have?*

Avere is used instead of **essere** in the following expressions.

avere fame (*to be hungry*); avere sete (*to be thirsty*); avere sonno (*to be sleepy*); avere caldo (*to feel hot*); averc freddo (*to feel cold*); avere ragionc (*to be right*); avere torto (*to be wrong*); avere paura (*to be scared/afraid*).

Hai fame? No, ho sete.   *Are you hungry? No, I am thirsty.*

Tu hai ragione ed io ho torto. *You are right and I am wrong.*

How old are you? I am … is translated:

  Quanti anni hai?   *How many years have you?*
   Ho … anni.   *I have … years.*

exercise

You have just visited the Simoni family in Sorrento and are telling your Italian friend about them. Translate the following into Italian.

Signor Simoni is writing a book. Signora Simoni has a lot of money and many clothes. They have a son and a daughter. Marianna, their daughter, has blond hair and blue eyes and a boat. She is twenty-three. She has many friends. Paolo, their son, is twenty. He has a new fast (**veloce**) car. They have a large house with an enormous garden. They also (**anche**) have a house in the country. Unfortunately (**Purtroppo**) they always have some (**dei**) problems.

41 andare, venire and uscire

Three more common irregular verbs.

	ANDARE *to go*	VENIRE *to come*	USCIRE *to go/to come out*
(io)	vado	vengo	esco
(tu)	vai	vieni	esci
(lui) (lei) (Lei)	va	viene	esce
(noi)	andiamo	veniamo	usciamo
(voi)	andate	venite	uscite
(loro) (Loro)	vanno	vengono	escono

I ragazzi vanno al bar.	*The boys go to the the bar.*
Vai al cinema?	*Are you going to the cinema?*
Chi va a fare la spesa?	*Who is going shopping?*
I signori Rossi vengono stasera?	*Are the Rossis coming this evening?*
Se viene Marianna io vado via.	*If Marianna comes, I go away.*
Da dove viene? Vengo da Pisa.	*Where do you come from? I come from Pisa.*
Vengo con te se non ti dispiace.	*I am coming with you if you don't mind.*
Di solito esco alle sette.	*I usually go out at seven.*
Quando esci?	*When do you go/are you going out?*

Quando esce dal bar gira destra. *When you go out of the bar you turn right.*

To say where you are from, you can either say **Vengo da …** (*I come from …*) or **Sono di …** (*I am from …*)

Vengo da/Sono di Barletta.   *I come from Barletta.*

exercise

Match the questions and answers.

a	Vai al cinema?	1	Di solito usciamo alle otto.
b	Esci?	2	Preferisco andare sola.
c	Da dove viene, signora?	3	Ci vanno Renzo e Lucia.
d	Vengono stasera i tuoi amici?	4	No, vado a teatro.
e	Vengo con te, ti dispiace?	5	No, andiamo oggi.
f	Uscite alle sette di solito?	6	Sì, esco.
g	Chi va a fare la spesa?	7	Vengo da Roma, e Lei?
h	Andiamo domani?	8	Vengono domani.

Translate the following into Italian.

i Who is going to the chemist?
j Where do you come from, madam?
k Where do you come from, Robert?
l Do you mind if (**se**) I come with you?
m I am going out.

Bere and **dire** are formed as if their infinitive forms were **bevere** and **dicere**. **Fare** is formed in yet another way.

	FARE *to do/to make*	BERE *to drink*	DIRE *to say/to tell*
(io)	faccio	bevo	dico
(tu)	fai	bevi	dici
(lui) (lei) (Lei) }	fa	beve	dice
(noi)	facciamo	beviamo	diciamo
(voi)	fate	bevete	dite
(loro) (Loro) }	fanno	bevono	dicono

A **Fare** translates *to do* and *to make*. As you know, Italian doesn't use *to do* to make either questions or the negative form.

To emphasize a verb, as in *I do speak Italian!*, you use expressions like **Certo che** (*certainly*) parlo italiano! *or* Vedo **bene!** (*I do see!*) Spero **proprio** (*really*) di venire! *I do hope to come!*

Isn't it?, Isn't she?, etc. are translated by **non è vero?**
Does he? Did he? etc. expressing surprise are expressed by **Davvero?** (*Really?*).

B **Fare** is also used in the following expressions: fare uno spuntino (*to have a snack*); fare la coda (*to queue*); fare una passeggiata (*to have a walk*); fare le valigie (*to pack*); fare il biglietto (*to buy the ticket*); fare colazione (*to have breakfast*); fare freddo (*to be cold (weather)*); fare due passi (*to have a stroll*); fare caldo (*to be hot (weather)*); fare una domanda (*to ask a question*).

Rifare (*to do again/to re-make*) is formed as **fare**.

C **Far fare** or **fare** + infinitive, preceded by the indirect object pronoun (**mi, ti, gli**, etc.), are used to translate *to have something done*.

Mi faccio fare un vestito.	*I'll have a dress made.*
Mi faccio tagliare i capelli.	*I am going to have my hair cut.*

exercise

Add the missing verb.

Eg. Paolo _____ soltanto vino rosso. → Paolo beve soltanto vino rosso.

a Noi non _____ alcolici. (*We do not drink alcohol.*)

b Loro _____ sempre le stesse cose. (*They always say the same things.*)

c _____ tutto alla mamma. (*We tell mum everything.*)

d Serafina _____ una torta. (*Serafina makes/is making a cake.*)

e La sera _____ due passi. (*We have a stroll in the evenings.*)

In Italian two verbs are used to translate *to know*: *sapere*, which is irregular, and *conoscere*, a regular verb. The main meaning of *dare* is *to give*.

	DARE *to give*	SAPERE *to know*
(io)	do	so
(tu)	dai	sai
(lui) (lei) } (Lei)	dà	sa
(noi)	diamo	sappiamo
(voi)	date	sapete
(loro/Loro)	danno	sanno

A Dare also translates:

• *to hold/have (a party)*
Sabato Marta dà una festa.
On Saturday Marta is giving a party.

• *to show (film)*
Che film danno oggi?
Which film are they showing today?

• *to perform* (a show, etc.)
Danno Amleto.
They're performing 'Hamlet'.

• *to think*
Quanti anni mi dai?
How old do you think I am?

The third person singular of **dare** always carries a grave (à) accent.

B **Sapere** is mainly used to express the knowledge of a fact.

So che Rita sposa John.	*I know that Rita is marrying John.*
Sai le notizie di oggi?	*Do you know today's news?*

It also means *to know how to do something* (*can you ...?*):

Sai cucinare?	*Can you cook?*

C **Conoscere** is mainly used for people and places.

Conosce il professor Rea?	*Do you know Professor Rea?*
Conosce Roma?	*Do you know Rome?*

Although **conoscere** is a regular verb (**conosco, conosci, conosce, conosciamo, conoscete, conoscono**), you need to pay attention to the pronunciation since -sc- is pronounced *sk* if it occurs before -**o** and *sh* before -**e** or -**i**.

exercise

Translate the following into Italian.

a How old do you think he is?
b What film is on television?
c The Simoni are organizing a party.
d Can you play (**giocare a**) tennis?
e He cannot play cards (**a carte**).
f They know that I cannot (**posso**) go.
g Will you give me your video?
h We do not know the truth.

As well as meaning *to stay*, and *to remain*, the verb *stare* has several other uses.

A **Stare** is also used:
- with health and exchanges of courtesies:

  Come sta, signora?
  How are you, madam?

  Oggi non sto molto bene.
  Today I am not very well.

	STARE *(to stay/to remain)*
(io)	sto
(tu)	stai
(lui) (lei) } (Lei)	sta
(noi)	stiamo
(voi)	state
(loro) } (Loro)	stanno

- to translate *to live/reside permanently or temporarily in a place*:

  Luigi sta con lei.   *Luigi lives with her.*
  Sto all'albergo.   *I live in the hotel.*
- to translate *to be situated*:

  Sta in cima al colle.   *It's on the top of the hill.*
- followed by **per** + infinitive to translate *to be about to do something*:

  Sto per uscire.   *I am about to go out.*
- followed by the gerund, to form the continuous form:

  Sta piovendo.   *It is raining.*
  In questo momento sto mangiando. *I am eating at the moment.*

B Note the verbal expressions where *to be* is translated by
stare: **stare attento** (*to be careful*); **stare zitto** (*to be silent*)
and **stare fermo** (*to stay still*).

Perché non stai attento?	*Why don't you pay attention/* *aren't you careful?*
Paolo non sta mai zitto.	*Paul is never quiet.*
Il bambino non sta mai fermo.	*The child is never still.*

C Other uses: **stare in piedi** (*to stand*); **stare alla cassa** (*to be at the till*); **stare a sentire** (*to listen*).

exercise

Match the questions and answers.

a Perché non stai attento
quando ti parlo?
b Come sta sua figlia?
c Com'è il tempo (*weather*)?
d Con chi abita Renato?
e Desidera sedersi?

1 Sta piovendo.
2 Sta con sua madre.
3 Perché sto leggendo in
questo momento.
4 No grazie, sto in piedi.
5 Sta bene grazie, e la sua?

Particular attention should be given to these three irregular verbs since they are constantly used.

	VOLERE *to want/to wish*	POTERE *can/to be able/may*	DOVERE *must/to have to*
(io)	voglio	posso	devo
(tu)	vuoi	puoi	devi
(lui) (lei) (Lei)	vuole	può	deve
(noi)	vogliamo	possiamo	dobbiamo
(voi)	volete	potete	dovete
(loro) (Loro)	vogliono	possono	devono

A Volere, dovere and potere are usually followed by an infinitive.

Voglio parlare al direttore.	*I want to speak to the manager.*
Puoi fare tutto quello che vuoi.	*You can do all you want.*
Devo partire.	*I must leave.*

B Volere may be followed by an object.

Voglio una Ferrari rossa.	*I want a red Ferrari.*

C The interrogative **Vuoi ...?/Volete ...?** (*Do you want ...?*) can also translate *Will you ...?* while **Posso ...?/Possiamo ...?** can mean *May I ...?/May we ...?*. **Devo ...?, Dobbiamo ...?** (*Must I ...?/Must we ...?*) can mean *Shall I ...?/Shall we ...?*

Vuoi/Volete venire in vacanza? *Will you come on holiday?*
Posso/Possiamo venire con te? *May I/we come with you?*
Devo/Dobbiamo venire anche noi? *Shall I/we come as well?*

Il potere (*the power*), **il volere** (*the will*), **il dovere** (*the duty*): these three words are nouns.

exercise

Insert the appropriate form of *volere*, *dovere* or *potere*.

a Noi non _____ fare quest'esercizio. **(potere)**
b Chi _____ leggere questo brano (*passage*)? **(volere)**
c Loro _____ ascoltare la radio. **(volere)**
d Marianna e Paolo _____ guardare la televisione. **(volere)**
e Noi non _____ vedere bene la lavagna (*board*). **(potere)**
f Lei non _____ parlare così, signore. **(dovere)**
g A chi _____ rivolgerci (*apply to/turn to*) noi? **(dovere)**
h Io _____ soltanto lavorare. **(dovere)**
i Tu _____ studiare di più. **(dovere)**

A few words on some technical terms to help identify some kinds of verbs.

A Transitive verbs imply an object. The action they express 'transits' from the subject to the object: **Leggo un libro** (*I read a book*). Even if I had only said *I read*, it would be understood that I (subject) read something (object). *To read* is therefore a transitive verb.

Intransitive verbs do not imply an object. With these verbs, the action stays with (or goes back to) the subject: **(Io) esco** (*I am going out*).

A simple test to see whether a verb is transitive or intransitive is to see if it can be followed by something that 'answers' the question *what?* or *who?*: **leggo** (*I am reading*) is transitive because I can ask *reading what?* and get the answer *a book, a magazine,* etc., whereas if I say **Il bambino dorme** (*The child sleeps*), the answer *sleeps what/who?* doesn't make sense. **Dormire** (*to sleep*) is therefore intransitive.

B Some verbs can be transitive or intransitive according to the way they are used. **Salgo le scale** (*I am going up the stairs*). The question *going up what?* is answered by *the stairs*, so **salire** in this case is transitive; **Salgo in camera** (*I am going up to my room*). This doesn't answer *what?* or *who?* and it is therefore intransitive.

C A verb, according to how it is related to the subject, can be either active or passive. The active form is when the subject carries out the action: **Battisti** (subject) **canta la**

canzone (*Battisti is singing the song*). The passive form is when the action is carried out by the object: **La canzone è cantata da Battisti** (object) (*The song is being sung by Battisti*). The meaning of the two forms is identical, although Italian tends to use the passive form far less than English.

As in English, the passive form is rendered by **essere** (*to be*) and the past participle, which agrees with the subject in gender and number.

D With simple tenses, **venire** can be used instead of **essere** to give the same meaning:

Il Chianti viene prodotto in Italia. *Chianti is produced in Italy.*

E Some common passive constructions use **si** (*one*) + third person singular or plural of the verb: Si parla italiano qui. *Italian is spoken here* (lit.: *One speaks Italian here*). This form unlike the English *one*, is much used in Italian.

exercises

Sort out which are transitive and which are intransitive verbs.
vedere dormire avere essere mangiare finire capire studiare piovere

Which sentences are active and which are passive?
a Io recito una poesia. b La poesia è recitata (*by*) me.
c L'auto viene fabbricata in Italia. d L'Italia produce pasta, olio e vino. e La scheda telefonica è usata da (*by*) molte persone. f La carta di credito viene emessa (*issued*) dalla (*by*) banca.

Reflexive verbs express an action that reflects back to the subject.

A In this verbal form, the subject and the object are the same person.

(io)	mi	lavo	*I wash myself*
(tu)	ti	lavi	*you wash yourself*
(lui/lei/Lei)	si	lava	*he/she washes him/herself/ you wash yourself (formal)*
(noi)	ci	laviamo	*we wash ourselves*
(voi)	vi	lavate	*you wash yourselves*
(loro/Loro)	si	lavano	*they wash themselves/ you wash yourselves (formal)*

B As in English, these are ordinary verbs but unlike English, they are preceded (rather than followed) by the reflexive pronoun. Reflexive pronouns behave like all the other direct and indirect object pronouns and are identical to them, except for the third persons singular and plural (**si**):

Mario si rade. *Mario is shaving (shaves himself).*
Loro si lavano. *They wash/are washing (themselves).*

C The reflexive infinitive is formed by replacing the final vowel of an ordinary infinitive with **-si: lavare** (*to wash*) → **lavarsi** (*to wash oneself*).

D Like **lavarsi** and **radersi**, several verbs are reflexive both in Italian and in English: **farsi male** (*to hurt oneself*), **divertirsi** (*to enjoy oneself*).

The English verbal form *to get* + past participle or adjective usually corresponds to an Italian reflexive verb:

prepararsi	(*to get ready*)	seccarsi	(*to get annoyed*)
vestirsi	(*to get dressed*)	stancarsi	(*to get tired*)
abbronzarsi	(*to get a tan*)	preoccuparsi	(*to get worried*)

Here are some common Italian reflexive verbs which are not reflexive in English: **chiamarsi** (*to be called*), **accorgersi** (*to realize*), **svegliarsi** (*to wake up*), **alzarsi** (*to get up*), **sentirsi** (*to feel*), **rivolgersi (a)** (*to apply to*).

Translate the sentences below into Italian.

a Marianna puts on her make-up (**truccarsi**).
b Ciccio doesn't get up (**alzarsi**) early (**presto**).

More cases where Italian uses verbs in the reflexive form.

A Italian tends to use a reflexive verb to indicate possession when referring to parts of the body, clothing and other personal effects because it is usual to say, for example, *the leg* or *a leg* rather than *my leg* as in English.

Luigi si è rotto una gamba sciando.	*Luigi broke his leg while skiing.*
Devo lavarmi i capelli.	*I must wash my hair.*

B The reflexive form is also used to express reciprocal action and to translate expressions like *each other, one another.*

Si telefonano ogni giorno.	*They ring each other every day.*
Si incontrano.	*They meet (each other).*
Dovete rispettarvi.	*You must respect one another.*

C Other uses. Observe these examples:

L'autobus si è fermato.	*The bus stopped (lit. itself).*
Maria ha fermato l'autobus.	*Maria stopped the bus.*
La porta si è aperta.	*The door opened (lit. itself).*
Maria ha aperto la porta.	*Maria opened the door.*

D Some verbs can be used reflexively or non-reflexively:

Ho dimenticato il passaporto/Mi sono dimenticato(-a) il passaporto.	*I forgot my passport.*
Ho riposato un'ora. Mi sono riposato(-a) un'ora.	*I had an hour's rest.*

E Reflexive pronouns preceded by a preposition are translated:

sé/se stesso (-a)	*oneself*	noi/noi stessi (-e)	*ourselves*
me/me stesso (-a)	*myself*	voi/voi stessi (-e)	*yourselves*
te/te stesso (-a)	*yourself*	sé/se stessi (-e)	*themselves*
sé/se stesso (-a)	*him/herself*		

Quella ragazza è piena di sé. *That girl is full of herself.*
Devi credere in te stesso. *You must believe in yourself.*

F Note this use of **stesso** (*oneself*).
Andrò io stesso. *I will go myself.*
Ha deciso lui stesso. *He himself decided.*

exercise

Cross out the possessive adjective when not needed.
E.g. Devo lavarmi i ~~miei~~ capelli

a Vuoi cambiarti la tua giacca?
b Mi metto (*put on*) il mio vestito.
c Ti sei lavato le tue mani?

Translate the following into Italian.

d The train stopped at Lucca.
e The window opened.
f Giulia opened the window.
g That man is full of himself.
h The car stopped and the door opened.
i The alarm (**allarme**) stopped the train.
j Giulia doesn't believe in herself.
k She herself went.

The past participle is an extremely useful part of the verb because, as in English, it is added to the auxiliaries *to be* and *to have* to make other tenses.

A These three examples use the auxiliary verb *to have* + the past participle:

ho parlato (*I have spoken*); ho venduto (*I have sold*); ho finito (*I have finished*)

Spoken, sold and *finished* are past participles. You form the past participle in the following way: **-are**, **-ere** and **-ire** become **-ato**, **-uto**, **-ito** respectively:

parlato (*spoken*); studiato (*studied*); imparato (*learned*); andato (*gone*); mangiato (*eaten*); dato (*given*); stato (*been*); avuto (*had*); venduto (*sold*); conosciuto (*known*); ripetuto (*repeated*); creduto (*believed*); partito (*left/departed*); udito (*heard*); sentito (*felt/heard*); capito (*understood*); bollito (*boiled*).

B All **-are** verbs have a regular past participle except **fare**. Most **-ere** and a few **-ire** past participles are irregular. The most common are:

aprire → aperto (*opened*)
bere → bevuto (*drunk*)
chiudere → chiuso (*closed/shut*)
correre → corso (*run*)
decidere → deciso (*decided*)
dire → detto (*said/told*)
essere → stato (*been*)

nascere → nato (*born*)
offrire → offerto (*offered*)
percorrere → percorso (*covered a distance*)
permettere → permesso (*allowed*)
prendere → preso (*taken/caught*)
rimanere → rimasto (*remained*)

fare → fatto (*done/made*)	rompere → rotto (*broken*)
leggere → letto (*read*)	scendere → sceso (*gone/come down*)
mettere → messo (*put*)	scrivere → scritto (*written*)
morire → morto (*dead*)	venire → venuto (*come*)
muovere → mosso (*moved*)	vivere → vissuto (*lived*)

Although **vedere** has a regular and an irregular past participle, **veduto** and **visto**, the latter is more common.

C The past participle can often be used as an adjective or as a noun:

un attore ben conosciuto	*a well-known actor*
Il ferito è in condizioni stazionarie.	*The injured man is in a stable condition.*

Some past participles are spelt exactly as some nouns with a completely different meaning: **letto** (*bed*), **corso** (*avenue*), **dato** (*datum*).

exercise

Translate into Italian.

a The shop is closed.
b The chemist is open.
c I have seen the film twice.
d I have written a letter.
e I have taken a house in Tuscany.
f I have made a cake (**torta**).
g She has lived well.
h I have allowed Marina to go out.
i I have read the book.
j I have walked three kilometres.

An important tense to learn. In Italian, it is called *passato prossimo* and it is used to talk about something that has happened in the past.

A It is formed by the present tense of **avere** or **essere** + past participle: Ho parlato. *I spoke/I have spoken.*
Sono partita. *I left/I have left (f).*
Abbiamo parlato tutto il giorno. *We have been talking all day.*

	PARLARE	PARTIRE
(io)	ho parlato	sono partito/partita
(tu)	hai parlato	sei partito/partita
(lui) (lei) (Lei)	ha parlato	è partito/partita
(noi)	abbiamo parlato	siamo partiti/partite
(voi)	avete parlato	siete partiti/partite
(loro/Loro)	hanno parlato	sono partiti/partite

B **Essere** is used instead of **avere** mainly (but not always) with verbs of motions or with verbs expressing a change in position or condition. Here are the most common verbs taking **essere**: andare, venire, arrivare, partire, scendere, salire, nascere, morire, fuggire, scappare, correre, ritornare, uscire, diventare, arrossire, stare, rimanere.

Mario è partito ieri.	*Mario left yesterday.*
Siamo usciti.	*We went out.*

Camminare (*to walk*) takes **avere**.

Other cases in which **essere** is used are:
- with reflexive verbs:
  Mi sono molto meravigliata. *I was very surprised.*
- with impersonal verbs:
  È stato necessario lavorare. *It was necessary to work.*

C Agreements. With **essere**, the past participle needs to agree in gender and number with the subject
Rosella è partita ieri. *Rosella left yesterday.*

This doesn't happen with **avere** unless the perfect is preceded by an object pronoun.

Abbiamo comprato due dischi.	*We have bought two records.*
Li abbiamo comprati.	*We have bought them.*

exercise
This is an extract from a girl's diary. Change the verbs in the present tense into the perfect.

E.g. Sono andata in vacanza …

(**a** Sono) in vacanza con Paolo, Liana e Francesco. Questa mattina Liana e Paolo (**b** vanno) al mare mentre (*while*) Francesco ed io (**c** andiamo) a Portofino a piedi; (**d** impieghiamo – *we take*) circa 50 minuti. (**e** Arriviamo) a Portofino e (**f** facciamo) il giro dei negozi, poi (**g** ci sediamo) in piazza, all'aperto, al tavolino di un bar e (**h** prendiamo) un cappuccino con un sandwich.

The Italian perfect tense can be used to translate the English perfect and simple past tenses.

A The Italian perfect tense (**passato prossimo**), as well as translating the English perfect (*I have spoken, I have gone*), is used – particularly in spoken Italian – to express an action started and ended in the past expressed in English by the simple past (*I spoke, I went*).

Ho capito. *I have understood/I understood.*
Avete fatto la spesa? *Have you done/Did you do the shopping?*
Anna è arrivata in tempo. *Anna has arrived/arrived on time.*

B The perfect tense is also used to translate *I have been …*
ho camminato (*I have been walking*)
ho vissuto (*I have been living*)

  Ho camminato tutto il giorno. *I have been walking all day.*
  Ho vissuto a Roma per sei mesi. *I have been living in Rome
                       for six months.*

The object pronoun precedes the auxiliary.
  Ho bevuto il caffè in fretta.   *I drank the coffee in a hurry.*
  L'ho bevuto in fretta.   *I drank it in a hurry*

C With **dovere, potere** and **volere**, the choice between the use of **essere** or **avere** depends on the following infinitive.

Sono dovuto **partire** (since **partire** takes **essere**) (*I had to leave*) but **ho** dovuto **camminare** (since **camminare** takes **avere**) (*I had to walk*).

exercises

Enter the correct auxiliary verb.

a Renzo _____ dovuto tornare indietro.
b Clara _____ voluta restare a Roma.
c Claudia non _____ potuto telefonare.
d Flavia non _____ potuta restare.
e I Simoni _____ voluto invitare Maria.
f Non _____ potuti andare al mare.
g (Noi) _____ guardato la partita di calcio alla TV.

Translate the following into Italian.

h I had to walk two miles.
i They had to leave early.
j Have you (*informal singular*) spoken to the (**al**) doctor?
k Did you go out yesterday evening?
l We watched the football match on TV.
m I saw him yesterday.
n They told her at once (**subito**).
o She rang him from (**da**) Naples (**Napoli**).
p They spoke to the (**al**) president.
q We have been living in India for three years.

The imperfect, also called the past descriptive, is the tense used to describe events which happened in the past.

The imperfect is a relatively easy tense to conjugate, with no irregular forms, except for **essere**. The stress falls on the underlined syllable.

	PARLARE	VENDERE	FINIRE	ESSERE
(io)	parl<u>a</u>vo	vend<u>e</u>vo	fin<u>i</u>vo	<u>e</u>ro
(tu)	parl<u>a</u>vi	vend<u>e</u>vi	fin<u>i</u>vi	<u>e</u>ri
(lui/lei/Lei)	parl<u>a</u>va	vend<u>e</u>va	fin<u>i</u>va	<u>e</u>ra
(noi)	parlav<u>a</u>mo	vendev<u>a</u>mo	finiv<u>a</u>mo	erav<u>a</u>mo
(voi)	parlav<u>a</u>te	vendev<u>a</u>te	finiv<u>a</u>te	erav<u>a</u>te
(loro/Loro)	parl<u>a</u>vano	vend<u>e</u>vano	fin<u>i</u>vano	<u>e</u>rano

A The imperfect is used to describe:
* a situation in the past: Era povero. *He was poor.*
* a repeated or habitual action carried out in the past (*I used to …; I would…*):
  Prendevo il treno tutti i giorni. *I took/used to/would take the train every day.*
  Leggevo molto. *I read/used to/would read a lot.*
* an action going on while something else happened or was happening (*I was …ing*); often the word **mentre** (*while*) introduces these sentences.
  Scrivevo quando ha telefonato. *I was writing when he rang.*

Mentre uscivo è arrivata la posta.	*The mail arrived while I was going out.*

B The compound tense of this verb, called the pluperfect, is formed by the imperfect of **essere** or **avere** + the past participle.

ero partito/a *I had left.*	avevo parlato *I had spoken.*
L'autobus era partito.	*The bus had left.*
Avevo visto quel film.	*I had seen that film.*
Erano partiti.	*They had left.*

exercise

Change the verbs in italics into the Italian imperfect form.

a Quando *I was* un teenager *I wanted* una Ferrari rossa.

b *I used to play* (**suonare**) le mie canzoni preferite al pianoforte ma non *was* molto brava.

c D'estate *I used to go* alla spiaggia ogni giorno.

d *I would swim* (**nuotare**) per ore ed ore.

e *I used to eat* continuamente.

f Mentre *I was studying, I listened* la radio, e *ate* torte.

g Prima di cena *I used to go out* con i miei amici.

h *We spoke* di tutto: teatro, musica, filosofia …

i Alle otto *I would return* a casa per la cena.

Impersonal verbs do not have a subject. They are verbs used only in the third person.

You can test to see if a verb is impersonal by trying to use other subject pronouns with it. **Piove** (*it's raining*) is impersonal because you can't say *I am raining*, *you are raining*, etc. The following verbs belong in this group.

A **bisognare/essere necessario/occorrere** + infinitive (*to be necessary*)

Bisogna/è necessario/occorre   *It's necessary to pay taxes.*
  pagare le tasse.

Do not confuse **bisogna** with **avere bisogno di ...** (*to have need of*):

Ho bisogno di un nuovo   *I need a new pair of shoes.*
  paio di scarpe.

B **volerci** + noun (*to be needed* and – with expressions of time – *to take*):

Ci vuole un sacco di pazienza.   *A lot of patience is needed.*
Quanto ci vuole?   *How long does it take?*

When **volerci** has a plural object, the third person plural must be used:

Quante ore ci vogliono?   *How many hours does it take?*

C **bastare** + infinitive or noun (*to suffice/to be enough*)

Per superare l'esame   *It is enough to study to pass*
  basta studiare.   *the exam.*

When **bastare** is followed by a plural object, the third person plural must be used:

Ne bastano duecento grammi. *Two hundred grams suffice.*

D **piacere** + noun or infinitive (*to like*). This verb is dealt with in the next unit.

E Verbs concerning the weather such as
piovere (*to rain*); piovigginare (*to drizzle*); nevicare (*to snow*); grandinare (*to hail*); lampeggiare (*to be lightning*); tuonare (*to thunder*); rasserenarsi (*to clear up*)

Oggi piove.   *It is raining today.*
Si è rasserenato.   *It has cleared up.*

exercise

Choose between *ci vuole* or *ci vogliono* and complete the following sentences. Read the whole sentence each time.

E.g. Per andare all'estero _____ il passaporto. → Per andare all'estero ci vuole il passaporto.

Per andare all'estero …   Per guidare la macchina …

a _____ la valigia.   d _____ la patente.

b _____ molti soldi.   e _____ molti litri di benzina.

c _____ il biglietto.   f _____ il libretto di circolazione.

The Italian verb *piacere* (to like) behaves differently from its English equivalent. Only the third person singular and plural (*piace* and *piacciono*) are used.

A In Italian, **piacere** is often used in the same way as *to be pleasing*; in this case it is therefore constructed impersonally (only in the third persons singular and plural).

Mi piace la musica.	*I like music (Music is pleasing to me).*
Mi piacciono i fiori.	*I like flowers (Flowers are pleasing to me).*

In other words, what in English is the subject in Italian becomes an indirect object: indirect object (**mi, ti, gli, ci, vi,** etc.) + **piacere** + subject.

Piacere can be followed by an infinitive, in which case the third person singular is used.

Mi piace camminare.   *I like walking.*

The negative **non** precedes the pronoun:

Non mi piace spettegolare.   *I don't like gossiping.*

Dispiacere means *to be sorry* and is used in the same way as **piacere**.

Mi dispiace molto.   *I'm very sorry.*

B The stressed pronoun is used for emphasis.

A me piace questo libro.   *I like this book.*

It must also be used when two indirect objects are involved.

A lui piace ma a me no.   *He likes it but I don't.*

If there is a noun or a name instead of **mi, ti, gli** etc. the following construction must be used:

A Paolo piace il polo.   *Paul likes polo.*
Agli italiani piace l'espresso.   *Italians like espresso coffee.*

C When **piacere** is conjugated normally, without the indirect object pronoun, it means *I am liked, you are liked*, etc. It has an irregular present: **piaccio, piaci, piace, piacciamo, piacete, piacciono** (past participle: **piaciuto**).

The perfect is formed with **essere.**

Vi è piaciuta la mostra?   *Did you like the exhibition?*

What would you like? in a bar or a restaurant is translated by **Che cosa prende(-i)?** When shopping, *I would like* is translated by **vorrei.**

exercise

Fill in the blanks using *piace* or *piacciono*.

a Mi _____ molto la storia.
b Vi _____ sciare?
c Ti _____ la musica pop?
d I tuoi dischi non mi _____ .
e A Paolo _____ le tagliatelle.
f Agli inglesi _____ visitare i musei.
g A me _____ i fiordalisi, a Cristina _____ le rose.
h Non ci _____ quel profumo.

The future tense is used to indicate an action that is still to happen.

	PARLARE	LEGGERE	PARTIRE	ESSERE	AVERE
(io)	parlerò	leggerò	partirò	sarò	avrò
(tu)	parlerai	leggerai	partirai	sarai	avrai
(lui/lei/Lei)	parlerà	leggerà	partirà	sarà	avrà
(noi)	parleremo	leggeremo	partiremo	saremo	avremo
(voi)	parlerete	leggerete	partirete	sarete	avrete
(loro/Loro)	parleranno	leggeranno	partiranno	saranno	avranno

A In Italian the future is used to express:
• an action still to happen:
  Presto gli scriverò.   *I will write to him soon.*
• a probability or a hypothesis:
  Paolo sarà fuori.   *Paul must be out.*
  Avrà perso il treno.   *He may have missed the train.*

B The present tense is often used, particularly in the spoken language, to indicate an action that is going to happen in the future, when English would use the continuous form.
  Domani gli parlo.   *Tomorrow I am going to speak to him.*

When *to be going to* expresses intention, it can be translated by **intendere** or **avere intenzione di** + infinitive.
  Ho intenzione di/Intendo   *I am going to leave*
    partire domani.   *tomorrow.*

To indicate an action about to happen, Italian uses **stare per**.
Sto per uscire.   *I am going out (I am about to go out).*

C Avere, andare, venire, dovere, potere, volere, vedere and
rimanere have a slightly shortened future form: **avrò…;
andrò…; verrò…; dovrò…; potrò…; vorrò…; vedrò…;
rimarrò…**

D The future perfect is formed using the future of **essere** or
avere + past participle. Avrò finito questo libro per
settembre. *I will have finished this book by September.*

Note these constructions:

Quando andrò a Roma ti telefonerò.	*When I go to Rome, I will ring you.*
Che cosa prendi? Prendo …	*What will you have? I will have …*

exercise

**Change these sentences into the future tense. Add *domani*
or *tra poco* ('in a short time') to either the beginning or the
end of your answer.**

E.g. Oggi esco. → Domani uscirò/Uscirò domani.
Gli parlo. → Gli parlerò domani/Domani gli parlerò.

a Leggo il libro.
b Il treno parte.
c L'autobus arriva.
d Studio la lezione.
e Vado a piedi.
f Rimango a casa.
g Le telefono.
h La vedo.

The conditional present tense is used to imply a condition or a possibility. It is also used for polite requests.

	PARLARE	SCRIVERE	FINIRE
(io)	parlerei	scriverei	finirei
(tu)	parleresti	scriveresti	finiresti
(lui/lei/Lei)	parlerebbe	scriverebbe	finirebbe
(noi)	parleremmo	scriveremmo	finiremmo
(voi)	parlereste	scrivereste	finireste
(loro/Loro)	parlerebbero	scriverebbero	finirebbero

A As in the future tense, the following verbs have a slightly shortened stem/ending combination in the conditional. The first person singular is given to indicate the pattern: avere → avrei; essere → sarei; andare → andrei; venire → verrei; dovere → dovrei; potere → potrei; volere → vorrei; vedere → vedrei; rimanere → rimarrei

Dovresti studiare di più. *You should study more.*

B The conditional present is used in the same way as in English to express a wish, request, opinion or intention.

Vorrei andare in vacanza. *I'd like to go on holiday.*
Io direi di sì. *I would agree.*
Aldo verrebbe ma non può. *Aldo would come, but he can't.*

C As in English, the conditional present is often linked with the conjunction **se** (*if*). In this construction Italian requires the imperfect subjunctive after *se*.

Andrei in vacanza se potessi. *I would go on holiday if I could.*

D *Ought to* is translated by **dovrei, dovresti**, etc. or **bisognerebbe**.

Dovresti essere contento.   *You ought to be glad/happy.*
Bisognerebbe dirglielo.   *One ought to tell him.*

E The difference between **mi piacerebbe** and **vorrei** is that the former is a mere wish: **Mi piacerebbe imparare il cinese** (*I'd like/love to learn Chinese*), whereas the latter is more positive and must be used when you are asking for directions, information or something in a shop, office, etc.

exercise

Answer the questions using the correct person of the verb.

E.g. Perché non parli? (ho mal di gola). → Parlerei ma ho mal di gola.

a Perché non studi? (sono stanca)
b Perché non scrivete? (non abbiamo tempo)
c Perché non finite? (è troppo tardi)
d Perché non partono? (non hanno i soldi)
e Perché non guardano la TV? (hanno altro da fare)
f Che fa tuo fratello, viene? (non ha tempo)

The conditional perfect tense is formed from the present conditional of *essere* or *avere* plus the past participle of the verb.

	ESSERE	AVERE
(io)	sarei stato/a	avrei avuto
(tu)	saresti stato/a	avresti avuto
(lui/lei/Lei)	sarebbe stato/a	avrebbe avuto
(noi)	saremmo stati/e	avremmo avuto
(voi)	sareste stati/e	avreste avuto
(loro/Loro)	sarebbero stati/e	avrebbero avuto

	PARLARE	VENDERE	PARTIRE
(io)	avrei parlato	avrei venduto	sarei partito/a
(tu)	avresti parlato	avresti venduto	saresti partito/a
(lui/lei/Lei)	avrebbe parlato	avrebbe venduto	sarebbe partito/a
(noi)	avremmo parlato	avremmo venduto	saremmo partiti/e
(voi)	avreste parlato	avreste venduto	sareste partiti/e
(loro/Loro)	avrebbero parlato	avrebbero venduto	sarebbero partiti/e

The conditional perfect is used:
• to express an intention, a possibility or a request made in the past:
  Avrei voluto fare domanda.   I *would have liked to apply.*
• with verbs like *to imagine, to feel, to believe, to think,* etc. when the main clause is in the past and the dependent clause refers to a later time (still in the past).

Credevo che sarebbe venuto. *I believed/thought that he would come.*

- to express uncertainty of some news not confirmed as a fact that happened in the past:

La signora X avrebbe   *Apparently Mrs X killed the*
assassinato il portiere.   *porter.*

The conditional perfect is often linked with an *if* clause which requires the pluperfect subjunctive:

L'avrei comprato se avessi avuto   *I'd have bought it if I had*
i soldi.   *had the money.*

I/you etc. had better … is translated: **farei/faresti meglio a +** infinitive. *I'd rather* is translated by **preferirei**.

exercise

Match the two halves of the sentences.

a	Sarei andata al Cairo ma …	1 … di essere trattato in tale maniera.
b	L'avrei comprato ma …	2 … è andato in Venezuela.
c	Sarei uscita ma …	3 … non volevo lasciarlo solo.
d	Il maggiordomo (*butler*) …	4 … non c'erano posti sull'aereo.
e	Avrei voluto vederlo ma …	5 … avrebbe ucciso (*killed*) la contessa.
f	Non avrei mai immaginato …	6 … non era in buone condizioni.

The imperative mood (*modo imperativo*) expresses a wish or a command that something be done.

	PARLARE	VENDERE	DORMIRE	ESSERE*	AVERE*
(tu)	parla	vendi	dormi	sii	abbi
(lui/lei/Lei)	parli	venda	dorma	sia	abbia
(noi)	parliamo	vendiamo	dormiamo	siamo	abbiamo
(voi)	parlate	vendete	dormite	siate	abbiate
(loro/Loro)	parlino	vendano	dormano	siano	abbiano

*Essere and avere are irregular verbs.

A This tense does not have the first person singular (*I*). The second and third persons singular of -**are** verbs have their own form.

Parla!   *Speak!*
Parli più lentamente, signora. *Speak more slowly, madam.*
Lui parli, noi lo ascolteremo. *Let him speak, we'll listen.*

All the other persons are borrowed from the present indicative or, in the case of the formal *you* (third person singular and plural), from the present subjunctive. The use of the subjunctive makes the formal *you* more of an exhortation rather than a command, but particularly with this tense, much depends on the tone of one's voice or on the context of what is being said:

Vada avanti dritto.   *Go straight on.*
Abbia pazienza!   *Bear with me!/Please do not bother me.*

B The negative for the second person singular (**tu**) uses the infinitive preceded by **non**.

Non vendere la casa, Paolo! *Do not sell the house, Paul!*

All the other forms take **non** before the affirmative form.

Non venda la casa, signora. *Do not sell the house, madam.*
Non uscite, ragazzi! *Do not go out, boys!*

C The direct and indirect object pronouns are attached to the end of the imperative except for the formal *you*, when they precede the imperative.

Comprala. *Buy it.* Non comprarla. *Do not buy it.*
Parlategli. *Speak to him.* Non parlatele. *Do not speak to her.*
Gli parli, signora. *Speak to him, madam.*
Glielo scriva. *Write (it) to him.*
Andiamoci. *Let's go there.* Non andiamoci. *Let's not go there.*

exercise

Replace the underlined names or nouns with the appropriate indirect object pronoun.

E.g. Manda il pacco <u>a Marianna</u>. → Mandale il pacco.
Telefona la notizia <u>a Paolo</u>. → Telefonagli la notizia.

a Scrivi (*tu*) la lettera <u>a Marcello</u>.
b Racconta (*tu*) tutto <u>a Goffredo</u>.
c Venda (*Lei*) la macchina <u>a Susanna</u>.
d Compri (*Lei*) un nuovo computer <u>a Sandro</u>.
e Consigli (*advise*) (*Lei*) <u>a Renzo</u> di stare a casa.
f Parlate (*voi*) del fatto <u>al presidente</u>.
g Mandate (*voi*) i documenti <u>al sindaco</u> (*mayor*).

As well as *essere* and *avere*, there are several other verbs that have irregular imperative forms.

	ANDARE	STARE	DARE	FARE	DIRE
(tu)	va'	sta'	da'	fa'	di'
(lui/lei/Lei)	vada	stia	dia	faccia	dica
(noi)	andiamo	stiamo	diamo	facciamo	diciamo
(voi)	andate	state	date	fate	dite
(loro/Loro)	vadano	stiano	diano	facciano	dicano

va' = vai, sta' = stai, da' = dai, fa' = fai. The form given in the table is the most commonly used.

A With these verbs, when the second person singular (*tu*) is followed by a pronoun, the first consonant of the pronoun is doubled except for the -**g** in **gli**.

Dammi quel libro, per favore.	*Give me that book, please.*
Dammelo, per favore.	*Give it to me, please.*
Fammi un favore.	*Do me a favour.*
Facci un caffè.	*Make us a coffee.*
Dagli una mano.	*Give him a hand.*

B *Go/come and see, go/come and take/buy*, etc. are translated by the verb of motion in the imperative form + **a** (*to*) + infinitive.

| Vieni a prendere un caffè. | *Come and have a cup of coffee.* |
| Vai a comprare il dolce. | *Go and buy the cake.* |

C The future imperative is formed by the future of the indicative mood as in English.

Farai come dico io!   *You will do as I say!*
Andrai domani!   *You will go tomorrow!*

exercises

1 Translate into Italian using the second person singular.

E.g. Stai attento(a)!

a Give her the book!
b Go away (**andare via**)!
c Tell the truth (**verità**)!
d Pay attention (**fare attenzione**)!
e Be quick (**fare presto**)!

2 Change the Italian version of the sentences above into the third person singular (*Lei*).

E.g. Stia attento/a.

3 Match the two columns bearing in mind that you use the *tu* form with Marianna and Paolo and the *Lei* form with her parents.

E.g. Ho detto a Marianna: 'Vieni domani'.

a Ho detto a Marianna: 1 'Vada tranquillo, io sto attenta a tutto.'
b Ho detto a Paolo: 2 'Sta' attento!'
c Ho detto al signor Simoni: 3 'Prestami (*lend me*) la tua borsa.'
d Ho detto alla signora Simoni: 4 'Mi faccia un favore.'

Rarely used in English, the subjunctive mood is used more in Italian, although at times it may be expressed by the future or the present indicative as in English.

A The subjunctive does not express a fact but a probability, a possibility, an uncertainty, a desire, a curse or an exhortation which often depends on an action expressed in the main clause: *We insist* (main clause) *that she go* (dependent clause). This verb often depends on the conjunction **che** (*that*). Also, since the first three persons singular have the same form, the subject pronoun is often used (to avoid confusion). This mood has two simple tenses (present and imperfect) and two compound tenses (perfect and pluperfect).

B The present subjunctive

	PARLARE	VENDERE	PARTIRE	FINIRE	ESSERE	AVERE
che io	parli	venda	parta	finisca	sia	abbia
che tu	parli	venda	parta	finisca	sia	abbia
che lui/lei/Lei	parli	venda	parta	finisca	sia	abbia
che noi	parliamo	vendiamo	partiamo	finiamo	siamo	abbiamo
che voi	parliate	vendiate	partiate	finiate	siate	abbiate
che loro/Loro	parlino	vendano	partano	finiscano	siano	abbiano

Spero che Renza telefoni presto.
Digli che venga.

I hope (that) Renza will ring soon.
Tell him to come.

C The subjunctive is used with conjunctions like **a meno che** (*unless*); **affinché** (*so that*); **benché/sebbene/quantunque** (*although*); **malgrado/nonostante** (*in spite of*); **a patto che/purché/a condizione che** (*as long as*); **prima che** (*before*); **senza che** (*without*); **nel caso che** (*in case of*); **supposto che** (*supposing*).

Benché abbia l'influenza   *Marco wants to go out*
Marco vuole uscire.   *although he has the flu.*

D When the subject in the main clause expressing hope, fear, desire, command, etc. is the same as that in the dependent clause, the construction is verb + **di** + infinitive.

Suppongo di avere ragione.   *I suppose I am right.*

E The perfect subjunctive is formed by the present subjunctive of **avere** or **essere** + the past participle of the verb.

Immagino che sia partito.   *I imagine he has left.*
Immagino che lui abbia perso   *I imagine (that) he has missed*
  il treno.   *the train.*

exercise

Change the underlined verb into the correct form of the present subjunctive.

a   Spero che lui mi **vendere** i biglietti per la partita di calcio.
b   Suppongo che lei **avere** ragione.
c   Penso che loro **partire** la settimana prossima.
d   Lo aiutano sebbene non lo **meritare**.
e   Spera che i Rossi gli **vendere** la villa.
f   Voglio uscire prima che **piovere**.

The initial vowel of the three regular verb endings is the same as the initial vowel of the three infinitives: *-are/-assi*, *-ere/ -essi*, *-ire/-issi*.

	PARLARE	VENDERE	PARTIRE	ESSERE	AVERE
che io	parlassi	vendessi	partissi	fossi	avessi
che tu	parlassi	vendessi	partissi	fossi	avessi
che lui/lei/Lei	parlasse	vendesse	partisse	fosse	avesse
che noi	parlassimo	vendessimo	partissimo	fossimo	avessimo
che voi	parlaste	vendeste	partiste	foste	aveste
che loro/Loro	parlassero	vendessero	partissero	fossero	avessero

A The pluperfect subjunctive is formed by the imperfect subjunctive of **essere** or **avere** + the past participle of the verb:

| Mario credeva che io fossi partita. | *Mario thought that I had left.* |
| Era importante che Mario fosse informato. | *It was important that Mario should be informed.* |

B If the verb in the main clause is in the past or in the conditional, it is followed by the imperfect subjunctive.

Pensavo che partisse.	*I thought that he was leaving.*
Vorrei che tu fossi qui.	*I wish you were here.*
Temevo che non venisse.	*I feared he wouldn't come.*
Ritornerebbe se avesse i soldi.	*He/She would return if he/she had the money.*

C As you can see in the examples above, the two actions happen at the same time. When the action of the subordinate clause occurs *before* that of the main clause e.g. *I thought* (main clause) *he had left* (subordinate clause), it is rendered by the pluperfect subjunctive.

Pensavo che fosse partito.	*I thought that he had left.*
Immaginavo che lo avessero trovato.	*I imagined that they had found it.*

D It may happen that a past action with no connection at all with the present has a present tense in the main clause.

Immagino che gli Etruschi fossero un popolo felice.	*I imagine that the Etruscans were a happy people.*

I wish, he/she etc. wishes …! can also be translated by **Magari fossi/fosse …!**

Magari fossi ricco(-a)!   *I wish I were rich!*

exercise

Change the underlined verb into the correct form of the imperfect subjunctive.

a Speravo che lui mi **vendere** i biglietti per la partita di calcio.
b Supponevo che lei **avere** ragione.
c Pensavo che loro **partire** la settimana prossima.
d Lo aiutavano sebbene non lo **meritare**.
e Sperava che i Rossi gli **vendere** la villa.
f Volevo uscire prima che **piovere**.
g Nonostante io **mangiare** moltissimo non ingrassavo.
h Credevo che la festa **avere** luogo domani.

The only way to get a feel for the use of this mood is with lots of practice in speaking, writing, reading and listening to it.

The subjunctive is mainly used:

A in an *if* clause when the verb in the main clause is in the conditional mood (in which case the imperfect or the pluperfect subjunctive is used).

Andrei in vacanza se ne avessi il tempo.	*I would go on holiday if I had the time.*
Sarei andato(-a) in vacanza se ne avessi avuto il tempo.	*I would have gone on holiday if I had had the time.*

B with verbs or expressions conveying personal opinion or something not certain, such as: **credere, immaginare, parere/sembrare** (*to seem*), **pensare/ritenere** (*to think/to deem*), **supporre; può darsi/può essere** (*may be*), **si dice** (*it is said*), **è possibile, è impossibile, è probabile, è improbabile.**

Si dice che sia un buon professore.	*He is said to be a good teacher.*
Si diceva che fosse un buon professore.	*It was said that he was a good teacher.*

With verbs expressing personal opinion, the subjunctive is not necessary if one is well convinced of one's own opinion.

Penso che Dio esiste.	*I think God exists.*

C with verbs or expressions of hope, will or fear such as: **sperare, volere, desiderare, preferire, augurarsi, avere paura/temere** (*to fear*), **insistere.**

Mi auguro che tu abbia ragione.	*I hope that you are right.*

D with verbs expressing feeling such as: **far piacere, dispiacere, essere lieto(-a), essere spiacente/rincrescere** (*to be sorry*).

Sono lieto che lui abbia   *I am glad that he has*
accettato il posto.   *accepted the job.*

E with verbs expressing judgment such as: **è necessario, bisogna, conviene, è bene, è male, è pericoloso, è giusto, è ingiusto, è stupido, è incredibile, è un peccato** (*it's a shame*), **è importante, è strano** (*it's strange*).

È strano che si comporti   *It's strange that he should*
così.   *behave so.*

F with conjunctions or expressions like: **benché/sebbene/ quantunque** (*although*), **malgrado/nonostante** (*in spite of*), **a patto che/a condizione che/purché** (*as long as*), **a meno che** (*unless*), **prima che, nel caso che, supposto che.**

Benché abbia ragione tace.   *Although s/he is right, s/he*
keeps silent.

exercise

Translate the following into Italian.

Note: *Should* in this context is not a conditional verb, but stands for the subjunctive. The bureaucratic-sounding phrase *I demand that he reply at once* becomes in ordinary English speech *I demand that he should reply at once.*

a They insisted that we should leave at once (**subito**).
b I fear that the child has caught a cold.
c I feared that the child had caught a cold.
d She is anxious (**Ci tiene molto**) that he should finish the job.

Below are some of the most common irregular subjunctives.

	STARE		DARE		FARE	
	present	imperfect	present	imperfect	present	imperfect
che io	stia	stessi	dia	dessi	faccia	facessi
che tu	stia	stessi	dia	dessi	faccia	facessi
che lui/lei/Lei	stia	stesse	dia	desse	faccia	facesse
che noi	stiamo	stessimo	diamo	dessimo	facciamo	facessimo
che voi	stiate	steste	diate	deste	facciate	faceste
che loro/Loro	stiano	stessero	diano	dessero	facciano	facessero

	ANDARE		DOVERE		POTERE	
	present	imperfect	present	imperfect	present	imperfect
che io	vada	andassi	debba	dovessi	possa	potessi
che tu	vada	andassi	debba	dovessi	possa	potessi
che lui/lei/Lei	vada	andasse	debba	dovesse	possa	potesse
che noi	andiamo	andassimo	dobbiamo	dovessimo	possiamo	potessimo
che voi	andiate	andaste	dobbiate	doveste	possiate	poteste
che loro/Loro	vadano	andassero	debbano	dovessero	possano	potessero

	VOLERE		VENIRE		DIRE	
	present	imperfect	present	imperfect	present	imperfect
che io	voglia	volessi	venga	venissi	dica	dicessi
che tu	voglia	volessi	venga	venissi	dica	dicessi
che lui/lei/Lei	voglia	volesse	venga	venisse	dica	dicesse
che noi	vogliamo	volessimo	veniamo	venissimo	diciamo	dicessimo
che voi	vogliate	voleste	veniate	veniste	diciate	diceste
che loro/Loro	vogliano	volessero	vengano	venissero	dicano	dicessero

	TOGLIERE		TENERE		USCIRE	
	present	imperfect	present	imperfect	present	imperfect
che io	tolga	togliessi	tenga	tenessi	esca	uscissi
che tu	tolga	togliessi	tenga	tenessi	esca	uscissi
che lui/lei/Lei	tolga	togliesse	tenga	tenesse	esca	uscisse
che noi	togliamo	togliessimo	teniamo	tenessimo	usciamo	uscissimo
che voi	togliate	toglieste	teniate	teneste	usciate	usciste
che loro/Loro	tolgano	togliessero	tengano	tenessero	escano	uscissero

exercises

Which verbs are in the present subjunctive and which in the imperfect subjunctive?

a Voglio che tu stia attento.
b Vorrei che voi steste più attenti.
c Credo che stiano sempre a casa.
d Credevo che stessero sempre a casa.
e Vorrei che deste una mano a Pietro.
f Spero che facciano presto.
g E se facessimo un bella gita …?
h Mario non vuole che sua moglie vada al mare.
i Vorrebbe che andasse in montagna.

Put the verbs in brackets into the subjunctive.

j Vorrei che i miei figli (*stayed*) a casa di più.
k Sarei molto contenta se ti (*removed*) le scarpe quando entri in casa.
l Credo che Marietta (*goes out*) con Filippo.
m Credevo che Marietta (*went out*) con Filippo.

Also called past historic, this tense is mainly used instead of the perfect in formal writing such as newspapers and books.

64 past definite tense

A The Italian past definite translates verb forms like *I went*, *I did*, *I spoke* which express actions started and ended in the past. More recently, the perfect (*I have been*, *I have done*, *I have spoken*) has been adopted in Italian to convey the meaning of both tenses, at least in the spoken language and in informal writing. Nevertheless you should at least be aware of the existence of the past definite in order to be able to recognize it when you read.

	PARLARE	VENDERE	PARTIRE	FINIRE
(io)	parlai	vendei/vendetti	partii	finii
(tu)	parlasti	vendesti	partisti	finisti
(lui/lei/Lei)	parlò	vendè/vendette	partì	finì
(noi)	parlammo	vendemmo	partimmo	finimmo
(voi)	parlaste	vendeste	partiste	finiste
(loro/Loro)	parlarono	venderono/vendettero	partirono	finirono

-Ere verbs have an alternative first and third person singular and third person plural. Both forms are correct, though the first form is preferable when the verb stem ends in **-t**: **potei/potè/poterono** rather than **potetti/potette/potettero**.

B A large number of verbs have an irregular past definite. Here are few of the most common ones.
essere: fui, fosti, fu, fummo, foste, furono
avere: ebbi, avesti, ebbe, avemmo, aveste, ebbero

dire: dissi, dicesti, disse, dicemmo, diceste, dissero
dare: diedi/detti, desti, diede/dette, demmo, deste,
diedero/dettero
stare: stetti, stesti, stette, stemmo, steste, stettero
fare: feci, facesti, fece, facemmo, faceste, fecero
venire: venni, venisti, venne, venimmo, veniste, vennero
bere: bevvi, bevesti, bevve, bevemmo, beveste, bevvero
potere: potei, potesti, potè, potemmo, poteste, poterono
volere: volli, volesti, volle, volemmo, voleste, vollero
dovere: dovetti, dovesti, dovette, dovemmo, doveste, dovettero
nascere: nacqui, nascesti, nacque, nascemmo, nasceste, nacquero

The use of **essere** and **avere** is mainly confined to the
compound tense (past anterior):

Dopo che ebbe finito partì. *After he had finished, he went.*
The past definite of **essere** is also used to form the passive.
  Il palazzo fu costruito ...   *The building was built ...*

exercise

Answer the questions with the help of the information in brackets.

E.g. Chi fu Dante? (Il padre della lingua italiana). → Dante fu
il padre della lingua italiana.
a Dove e quando nacque Garibaldi? (a Nizza nel 1807)
b Quando dovette fuggire in Sud America? (dopo che ebbe
  partecipato ad un attentato (*attack*) per conquistare Genova)
c Che cosa fece quando ritornò? (partecipò alla lotta per
  l'Unità d'Italia)

65 which past tense?

The perfect, the imperfect, the pluperfect and the past definite can sometimes be found in the same sentence. This unit shows the four tenses working together.

While the imperfect expresses an action either going on or repeated in the past (= what was happening or used to happen), the perfect and the past definite express an action that started and ended (either at once or within a period of time) in the past (= what happened), while the pluperfect (formed from the imperfect of **essere** or **avere** plus past participle) expresses an action which took place before another event in the past.

In everyday speech you can safely use the perfect instead of the past definite but the former should express an action bearing some connection with the present while the latter should express an action completely removed from it:

Paolo è nato nel 1975. *Paul was born in 1975.* (he is still living – perfect).
Michelangelo nacque nel 1475. *Michelangelo was born in 1475.* (dead a long time – past definite).

You say: Ho appena comprato questo libro. *I've just bought this book.*
You could say: Ho comprato questo libro tre anni fa. *I bought this book three years ago.* (you still have it, maybe you are re-reading it now, or it is part of your library, a fact that bears some relation with the present, even if you had bought it thirty years ago).

But you can equally say: Comprai questo libro tre anni fa. *I bought this book three years ago* (here the emphasis is on the starting and ending of the action which happened three years ago).

When referring to distant events or historic facts and telling stories, the past definite is a must. Observe the verbs in the passage in the exercise below, where the past definite (past action) interacts with the imperfect (background action), the perfect (which is action still 'current') and the pluperfect (action preceding the background action).

exercise

Work out which tenses the verbs are in.

Si alzò dalla scrivania e si avvicinò al pianoforte. Non riusciva più a scrivere, pensò. Osservò la stanza: i fiori erano appassiti, i mobili avevano accumulato un velo di polvere. Cominciò a suonare pensando agli ultimi avvenimenti che avevano tanto cambiato la sua vita. Non si accorse che intanto faceva buio. Suonò per ore. A tarda notte si alzò dal pianoforte e salì in camera a fare le valigie. Da quel giorno non ha più scritto nulla.

He rose from his desk and approached the piano. He could not write a word, he thought. He slowly surveyed the room: the flowers had withered, the furniture had gathered a thin layer of dust. He started playing, thinking about the recent events that had changed his life so much. He did not realize it was getting dark. He played for hours. In the middle of the night he got up from the piano and went up to his room to pack. From that day he has written nothing.

Not all English words ending in *-ing* have the same function: some function as verbs, some as nouns and others as adjectives.

A When an *-ing* word is used as a verb it is known as the gerund. This is formed in Italian by replacing the infinitive endings **-are**, **-ere**, and **-ire** with **-ando**, **-endo** and **-endo** respectively.

PARLARE	VENDERE	PARTIRE	ESSERE	AVERE
parlando	vendendo	partendo	essendo	avendo

The gerund has only one form and it doesn't have to agree with the subject.

Partendo alle otto potrei   *(By) Leaving at 8 o'clock I*
arrivare prima.   *could arrive earlier.*

Irregular gerunds: dire → dicendo, fare → facendo, bere → bevendo

B The compound tense is formed by **essendo** or **avendo** + past participle …

Essendo partita alle otto   *Having left at 8 o'clock I*
sono arrivata prima.   *arrived earlier.*

… but it is not greatly used, and expressions like these are favoured:

Siccome (*Since*) sono partita alle otto sono arrivata presto.
Sono arrivata presto perché sono partita alle otto.

Object pronouns are added to the end of the gerund.

Avendolo comprato, decisi di usarlo.	*Having bought it, I decided to use it.*

C The gerund expresses the manner in which an action happens.

Ascolto spesso la musica scrivendo.	*I often listen to music when writing.*

It is also used to translate *by*, *while*, *in*, *since*, etc. + *-ing* ...

Avendo finito il compito sono uscito.	*After having finished my homework, I went out.*

... but equally you can say: Dopo che avevo finito il compito sono uscito.

D The progressive tense is formed by **stare** + gerund.

Non mi parlare adesso, sto leggendo.	*Do not speak to me now, I am reading.*

Andare + gerund gives a progressive form which expresses an unfolding or the repetition of an action.

La situazione andava peggiorando.	*The situation was worsening.*

exercise

Change the infinitives in brackets into gerunds.

a Non si risolvono i problemi (parlare).

b (Sbagliare) s'impara.

c Si è comprato la casa (lavorare) sodo (*hard*).

d (Continuare) così ti prenderai un esaurimento nervoso.

e (Avere) perso il treno chiamò un tassì.

This part of the verb (present participle) translates those *-ing* ending verbs which have an adjectival or a nominal function.

A The present participle in Italian is formed by replacing **-are**, **-ere** and **-ire** with **-ante**, **-ente** and **-ente** respectively.

PARLARE	CONTENERE	PARTIRE	ESSERE	AVERE
parlante	contenente	partente	essente/ente	avente/abbiente

Essente is very rarely used; **abbiente** can mean *s/he who owns* (i.e. someone rich).

B The present participle is very rarely used in Italian except:
• as an adjective:
  acqua bollente (*boiling water*); l'anno seguente (*the following year*)
• when it stands for a relative clause (*which*):

| Le uova sono un cibo nutriente (= che nutre). | *Eggs are a nourishing food.* |
| Il treno proveniente da Roma è in arrivo sul secondo binario. | *The train (coming) from Rome is arriving on platform two.* |

When in doubt, it is safer to use a relative clause:

| Sto leggendo una relazione riguardante (= che riguarda) la scuola. | *I am reading a report concerning (= that concerns) the school.* |

C Some Italian present participles have the value of a noun.
cantante (*singer*); insegnante (*teacher*); amante (*lover*);
studente (*student*); concorrente (*competitor*); dipendente
(*employee*); dirigente (*manager*); emigrante (*emigrant*).

D Many nouns which include an -*ing* form in English are
expressed differently in Italian: canna da pesca (*fishing rod*);
casa di cura/clinica (*nursing home*); carrozza letto (*sleeping
car*); piscina (*swimming pool*); carrozza ristorante (*dining
car*); sala da pranzo (*dining room*); lavatrice (*washing
machine*); salotto (*sitting room*); macchina da cucire (*sewing
machine*); sala d'aspetto (*waiting room*).

E Verbal nouns such as: *fishing, swimming, drinking,
writing, travelling, reading, painting,* etc. are rendered in
Italian by the infinitive.

Mi piace scrivere.	*I like writing.*
Vado a nuotare.	*I am going swimming.*

exercise

Translate the following using present participles/adjectives.

a Paolo is always (**sempre**) smiling.

b Francesco is a rich man.

c Is this the train from Rome?

d It was an amusing film.

e Do you know Maria's lover?

f Giovanni is a brilliant student.

g the rising sun

h the waning moon

Other -ing words are translated in Italian by the infinitive.

A -*ing* verbs are translated with an infinitive when:

• an -*ing* form has the function of a noun. In this case, the infinitive may even be preceded by the definite article.

(L') aiutare gli amici è lo scopo della sua vita. *Helping his friends is the main purpose of his life.*

• after a preposition, in which case the preposition is followed by the definite article.

Con l'andare del tempo si dimenticano molte cose. *With the passing of time one forgets many things.*

• with the prepositions **prima di** (*before*); **senza** (*without*); **oltre a** (*besides*); **invece di** (*instead*) and **dopo** (*after*).

Le telefonò prima di uscire. *He rang her before going out.*

Parlò senza alzare la testa. *He spoke without raising his head.*

In this case, **dopo** is followed by the infinitive of **avere** or **essere** + a past participle:

Dopo avere cenato pagò il conto e uscì. *After having dined, she paid and went out.*

To express purpose (*in order to*), **per** is used:

Lavora per comprarsi una casa. *He works (in order) to buy himself a house.*

B *To go* + -*ing* is often translated by **andare a** + infinitive.

Vado a ballare tutte le domeniche. *I go dancing every Sunday.*

Il sabato vado a pescare.   *I go fishing on Saturdays.*
Il venerdì vado a nuotare.   *I go swimming on Fridays.*

C Here is a list of English verbs + preposition + -*ing* verb which in Italian need to be followed by an infinitive.
to be used to (essere abituato a); *to be tired of* (essere stanco di); *to be on the point of* (essere sul punto di); *to thank for* (ringraziare di); *to think of* (pensare di); *to succeed in* (riuscire a); *to look forward to* (non vedere l'ora di).

exercises

Choose a suitable verb from the box to complete these sentences.

fumare	parlare	vivere	spendere
venire	pensare	continuare	

a Il _____ civile impone delle regole (*rules*) ben precise.
b (Il) _____ ad alta voce non è molto socievole.
c (Lo) _____ più di quanto si ha non è molto saggio.
d (Il) _____ troppo non giova alla salute (*doesn't help health*).
e Invece di _____ domani perché non vieni oggi?
f Invece di _____ a lamentarti perché non fai qualcosa?
g Non devi parlare senza _____ .

Some infinitives end in -urre, -orre and -arre. These belong to the second conjugation (-ere).

A Verbs ending in **-urre** come from the old form ending in **-ucere**.

produrre (*to produce*); tradurre (*to translate*); ridurre (*to reduce*); dedurre (*to deduce*); introdurre (*to introduce/insert*); riprodurre (*to reproduce*).

Verbs ending in **-orre** come from the old form ending in **-onere**:

porre (*to place/put/lay*); comporre (*to compose*), esporre (*to expose/exhibit*); disporre (*to dispose/arrange*); proporre (*to propose*).

Verbs ending in **-arre** come from the old form ending in **-aggere**:

trarre (*to draw*); contrarre (*to contract*); attrarre (*to attract*); distrarre (*to distract*); estrarre (*to extract*).

B These verbs have regular endings but slight variations in their stems. Each of the three groups behaves in the same way.

infinitive	PRODURRE	PORRE	TRARRE
present indicative	produco, produci, produce, produciamo, producete, producono	pongo, poni, pone, poniamo, ponete, pongono	traggo, trai, trae, traiamo, traete, traggono

imperfect	producevo, etc.	ponevo, etc.	traevo, etc.
future	produrrò, produrrai, produrrà, produrremo, produrrete, produrranno	porrò, porrai, porrà, porremo, porrete, porranno	trarrò, trarrai, trarrà, trarremo, trarrete, trarranno
past definite	produssi, producesti, produsse, producemmo, produceste, produssero	posi, ponesti, pose, ponemmo, poneste, posero	trassi, traesti, trasse, traemmo, traeste, trassero
present subjunctive	produca, etc.	ponga, ponga, ponga, poniamo, poniate pongano	tragga, tragga, tragga, traiamo, traiate, traggano
imperfect subjunctive	producessi, etc.	ponessi, etc.	traessi, etc.
conditional	produrrei, etc.	porrei, etc.	trarrei, etc.
imperative	produci, etc.	poni, ponga, poniamo, ponete, pongano	trai, tragga, traiamo, traete, traggano
past participle	prodotto	posto	tratto
gerund	producendo	ponendo	traendo

exercise

Write out the following verbs.

a the present tense of **comporre**
b the past definite of **attrarre**
c the imperative of **tradurre**
d the present tense of **tradurre**

Si, ci and *vi* are words with several different meanings. Below is a summary of their uses.

A Si

- Reflexive (third person singular and plural) and reciprocal pronoun.

  Mario si è rotto una gamba.   *Mario broke his leg* (reflexive).
  Si amano molto.   *They love each other a lot* (reciprocal).

Si becomes **se** before direct object pronouns **lo**, **la**, **li** and **le** and before **ne**:

  si lava la faccia = se la lava.   *he washes his face = he washes it.*

The reflexive form of **andare** is **andarsene** (*to go away/off*).
  Vorrei che se ne andasse.   *I wish her/him to go away.*
  Devo andarmene.   *I must be going.*

The above form can be used with other verbs to give an emphatic meaning to the action expressed by the verb:
  Si è mangiato la torta.   *He ate the cake (all by himself).*
  Se l'è mangiata tutta.   *He ate it all.*
- Impersonal pronoun: Si dice che sia ricco. *He is said to be rich.*
- Passive constructions: Qui non si fa credito. *Credit is not allowed here.*

B Ci/Vi

- Direct and indirect object pronouns meaning *us*, *to us/you*, *to you* (plural).
  Ci vieni a trovare?   *Will you come and see us?*

Vi ho scritto molte lettere.　　*I wrote (to) you many letters.*

All direct object pronouns can be added to **ecco**: **eccoci**, **eccomi**, **eccolo**, etc. meaning *here we are*, *here I am*, *here he/it is*, etc.

* Reflexive pronouns (ourselves/yourselves):
  Ci siamo divertiti.　　　　*We enjoyed ourselves.*
* Instead of **si** to make the impersonal form when the verb is reflexive.
  Quando ci si sveglia　　　*When one wakes up in*
   la mattina …　　　　　　*the morning …*
* Reciprocal pronouns (*each other*).
  Ci telefoniamo ogni giorno.　*We ring each other every day.*
* Adverb: **qui/qua** (*here*); **là/lì** (*there*).
  Ci sono stata.　　　　　　*I have been here/there.*

Vi can be used instead of **ci**, especially in writing.

* In spoken Italian you will hear people adding **ci** before **avere**.
  Ci ho tre figli.　　　　　*I have three sons.*
* With **credere** and **pensare**:
  Non ci credo.　　　　　　*I do not believe (in) it.*

exercise

Change the noun (and article) used as an object into the correct pronoun.

E.g. Si lava la camicia. → Se la lava.

a　Si fa il letto.　　　　　　c　Si prepara la cena.
b　Si fa la spesa.　　　　　　d　Si stira i pantaloni.

Sometimes a verb is followed by an infinitive, and the two verbs either follow each other directly or are linked with the prepositions *a* or *di*.

A Observe these three sentences:

Mi piace uscire.	*I like **going** out.*
Intendo uscire.	*I intend **to go** out.*
Devo uscire.	*I must **go** out.*

In each sentence, there are two verbs one after the other; all the English verbs in bold appear to have different forms (*going, to go, go*). In Italian, the second verb is usually an infinitive which may just follow the previous verb or be linked to it by a preposition (usually **a** or **di**).

Ho iniziato a studiare arte.	*I have started to study art.*
Cerca di capire.	*Try to understand.*

B Infinitives may also follow nouns and adjectives:

Non ha l'opportunità di viaggiare.	*He doesn't have the opportunity to travel.*
Sono sicuro di superare l'esame.	*I'm sure to pass the exam.*

Some verbs can be linked by the prepositions **con** (*with*) or **per** (*for/in order to*).

Ha finito con l'accettare le loro condizioni.	*He ended up by accepting their conditions.*
Venne da me per chiedere un'informazione.	*She came to ask for some information.*

C Below is a list of common verbs which do not need any preposition when followed by an infinitive.

amare (*to love/like*); ascoltare (*to listen to*); bastare (*to be enough*); bisognare (*to be necessary*); desiderare (*to wish/want*); detestare (*to detest*); dovere (*must/to have to*); fare (*to do/make*); guardare (*to look at*); importare (*to matter*); occorrere (*to be necessary*); odiare (*to hate*); osare (*to dare*); potere (*to be able to*); preferire (*to prefer*); sapere (*to know/know how to do something*); sentire (*to hear/listen to*); servire (*to serve/be of use*); vedere (*to see*); volere (*to want*)

Sai nuotare?	*Can you swim?*
Amo dipingere.	*I love painting.*

exercise

Match the two halves of the sentences.

a Come osi ...	1 ... vedere quanto è bello.
b Bisogna lasciarlo ...	2 ... piangere (*cry*) sul latte versato.
c Per superare gli esami ...	3 ... sapere dove ho messo gli occhiali.
d Detesto dover ...	4 ... cantare gli uccelli.
e Mi piace sentire ...	5 ... fare tutto in fretta.
f Vorrei ...	6 ... basta studiare.
g Non serve ...	7 ... fare come desidera.
h Dovresti ...	8 ... dire una cosa simile?

Some of the most common verbs take a preposition when they occur before an infinitive.

A verb + **a** + infinitive

affrettarsi a (*to hasten to*); aiutare a (*to help to*); autorizzare a (*to authorize to*); avere ragione a (*to be right to/in -ing*); avere torto a (*to be wrong to/in -ing*); cominciare a (*to start to*); continuare a (*to continue to/to go on -ing*); convincere a (*to convince (someone) to*); costringere a (*to force (someone) to*); esitare a (*to hesitate to*); fare meglio a (*to do better to*); imparare a (*to learn to*); impegnarsi a (*to undertake to*); incitare a (*to urge to*); incoraggiare a (*to encourage to*); indurre a (*to induce to*); invitare a (*to invite to*); mettersi a (*to set out to*); obbligare a (*to oblige to*); ostinarsi a (*to persist in -ing*); persuadere a (*to persuade to*); prepararsi a (*to get ready to*); provare a (*to try to*); rinunciare a (*to renounce to*); seguitare a (*to keep on -ing*); servire a (*to serve to/to be used for + -ing*); tardare a (*to be late in -ing*); tenerci a (*to be keen on -ing*); venire a (*to come to/come and*)

The preposition **a** acquires a **d** before a vowel.

Si fermò ad osservare il panorama. *She stopped to see the view.*

B verb + **di** + infinitive

accettare di (*to accept*); accorgersi di (*to realize*); avere bisogno di (*to need to*); avere intenzione di (*to intend to*); avere paura di (*to be afraid to*); avere vergogna di (*to be ashamed to*); avere voglia di (*to feel like -ing*); cercare di (*to try to*); cessare di (*to stop -ing*); chiedere di (*to ask (someone) to*); consigliare di (*to suggest -ing*); credere di (*to believe*); decidere di (*to decide to*); dire di (*to tell (someone) to*); essere contento di (*to be happy to*); essere sicuro di (*to be sure of -ing*); essere stanco di (*to be tired of -ing*); essere stufo di (*to be sick and tired of -ing*); fingere di (*to pretend to*); finire di (*to finish -ing*); giurare di (*to swear to*); immaginare di (*to imagine*); non vedere l'ora di (*to look forward to -ing*); pensare di (*to think of -ing*); permettere di (*to allow to*); pregare di (*to beg to*); pretendere di (*to claim to*); proibire di (*to forbid to*); promettere di (*to promise to*); proporre di (*to propose/suggest -ing*); raccomandare di (*to urge (someone) to*); rendersi conto di (*to realize*); ricordare di (*to remember to*); rifiutarsi di (*to refuse to*); sentirsela di (*to be willing to/have the strength of -ing*); sopportare di (*to bear to /-ing*); smettere di (*to give up -ing*); sognare di (*to dream of -ing*); sperare di (*to hope to*), tentare di (*to try/attempt to*); vantarsi di (*to boast of/about -ing*); vietare di (*to forbid to*)

exercise

Using the verbs above translate into Italian.

a Teresa is learning to play the piano.
b Paul is very keen on playing tennis.
c I am looking forward to seeing you.
d We are sick and tired of translating these exercises.
e They were sure to be right.

Prepositions locate, in position or time, a person/object in relation to another person/object. They are words like *with*, *at*, *to*, *by*, *from*, *of*, *about*, etc.

A Since Italian prepositions are not always translated with their nominal English counterparts, it is important to learn their use. In Italian it is sometimes possible to choose between two prepositions to convey the same meaning:

Sono a casa/Sono in casa.   *I am at home.*

When the definite article follows **di, a, da, in, su** it combines with it, e.g. **a + il = al**. **Con** may combine, but modern Italian tends to combine it mainly with **il** (= **col**) if at all.

B Con (*with*)

Vado a Roma con Paolo.	*I am going to Rome with Paul.*
Un tè con latte ma senza zucchero.	*A tea with milk but without sugar.*

Con also translates *by* when associated with means of transport.

Vado a Roma con l'aereo/ con il treno/con il pullman.	*I am going to Rome by air/train/coach.*

In this context, **in** can also be used: **in aereo/in treno/in pullman**.

C Other uses of **con** are when it conveys the meaning of:
• cause

Con questo caldo è difficile lavorare.	*It's difficult to work in this heat.*

- *against* (particularly with words like *fighting, at war* etc.)

  È come lottare con i mulini   *It is like fighting against*
  a vento.   *windmills.*

- *out of*

  Ho fatto queste tende con   *I made these curtains out*
  un vecchio copriletto.   *of an old bed cover.*

- *in spite of*

  Con tutti gli amici che ha è *In spite of the many friends*
  andato solo.   *he has, he went by himself.*

- *to*

  È sempre molto gentile con me. *He is always very kind to me.*
  con mia grande sorpresa   *to my great surprise*

Useful expressions: prenderla con calma *to take it calmly*;
prendersela con calma *to dawdle over something*

exercise

Rearrange the words to make meaningful sentences.

a lavorare difficile con rumore (*noise*) questo è
b prendo zucchero due caffè cucchiaini (*teaspoon*) il con di
c è arrivato Paolo madre sua l'automobile con di
d Marianna loro è con gentile stata
e Eleonora di ha andare la sua deciso con al cinema amica
f ha l'invito con accettato sorpresa mia grande
g dovrebbero a imparare calma con prenderla
h al con cinema lui andata ieri sono

As well as *of*, *di* in some cases translates *from* or *by*, or it can be used in other expressions as explained below.

di +	il	lo	la	l'	i	gli	le
=	del	dello	della	dell'	dei	degli	delle

Parlano di sport.   *They are talking about sport.*
Da questa finestra c'è una   *From this window there is a*
  bella vista della città.   *lovely view of the town.*

A Di + article is used to express an unspecified quantity:
Ha del pane?   *Have you any bread?*
Ho del pane bianco e del   *I have some white and*
  pane integrale.   *some brown bread.*

B Di is also used to indicate:
• possession: i giocattoli dei bambini *the children's toys*
• specification: l'arrivo del treno *the arrival of the train*
• denomination: la città di Venezia *the city of Venice*
• origin: Sono di Genova. *I am from Genoa.*
Where you are from is expressed by either **Sono di ...** or
Vengo da ...

• authorship (*by*): un libro di Rea *a book by Rea*
• content: una tazza di tè *a cup of tea*
• what something is made of: una cravatta di seta *a silk tie*
• ailments: Soffre di lombaggine. *He suffers from lumbago.*
• comparisons: Mio padre è più grande del tuo. *My father is bigger than yours.*

- time: di giorno *during the day*; di notte *during the night/at night*; di mattina/di sera *in the morning/evening*; di sabato *on Saturdays*; di ora in ora *hour by hour*; di giorno in giorno *day by day*
- after **qualcosa** and **niente** + adjective
  Vorrei qualcosa di meno caro. *I'd like something less expensive.*
  Non c'è niente d'interessante. *There is nothing interesting.*

C Note these phrases and expressions:

di solito	*usually*
Mi è caduto di mano.	*It fell from my hands.*
È il più grande cantante del mondo.	*He is the greatest singer in the world.*

exercise

Write the combined preposition and articles *del, dello, della* etc. in the blanks.

a L'amica _____ mamma ha telefonato da Miami.

b Da questa finestra c'è una bella vista _____ mare (*m.*).

c La gente _____ zona è molto simpatica e interessante.

d Vorrei _____ carciofi (*artichokes*), _____ zucchini (*courgettes*) e _____ mele.

e L'arrivo _____ nave (*f.*) è il 18 agosto.

f L'inizio _____ spettacolo è alle 21.15.

g Questo è un quadro _____ famoso pittore italiano Grignani.

h Quello che vedi laggiù è lo yacht _____ signora Marini.

The preposition *a* can mean *to, at, in, on*. It combines with the definite article.

a +	il	lo	la	l'	i	gli	le
=	al	allo	alla	all'	ai	agli	alle

Ho dato il libro a Roberto.   *I gave the book to Roberto.*

A A is used with:
- position. When referring to cities, towns, villages and small islands, **a** expresses both a motion toward a place (e.g. **vado a …**) or being in a place (e.g. **sono a …**).
  Vado a Pisa. *I am going to Pisa.* Vado a Capri. *I am going to Capri.*
  Sono a Pisa. *I am in Pisa.* Abito a Capri. *I live in Capri.*

Also: a casa (*home/at home*); al mare (*at/to the seaside*); alla spiaggia (*at/to the beach*); a cena (*at/to dinner*); al ristorante (*at/to the restaurant*); al bar (*at/to the bar*); all'aperto (*in the open air*); alla stazione (*at/to the station*); al porto (*at/to the port*); all'aeroporto (*at/to the airport*); alla televisione (*on television*); al cinema (*at/to the cinema*); a teatro (*at/to the theatre*)

- time: alle sei (*at six*); a mezzogiorno (*at midday*); a mezzanotte (*at midnight*); all'alba (*at dawn*); al tramonto (*at sunset*)
- age: A vent'anni si è sposato. *He married at twenty.*
- manner:
  Mi piace la pasta al pesto.   *I like pasta with pesto.*

un uovo alla coque	*a boiled egg*
Ho preso un libro a caso.	*I took a book at random.*
all'italiana	*Italian style*

- means:

| Vado a piedi. | *I go on foot.* |
| È fatto a macchina. | *It is made by machine.* |

B In Italian, **ascoltare** (*to listen to*), **guardare** (*to look at/to watch*), **additare** (*to point at*) and **fissare** (*to stare at/to gaze at*) are not followed by a preposition.

| Ascolto la radio. | *I listen to the radio.* |
| Guardo il panorama. | *I look at the view.* |

exercise

Where are these people going?

a Il bambino sta andando _____ .
b Il tassì sta andando _____ .
c La famiglia sta andando _____ .

In translates *to, in, by, within.* **It combines with the definite article.**

in +	il	lo	la	l'	i	gli	le
=	nel	nello	nella	nell'	nei	negli	nelle

A **In** is used with:
- position (both movement toward (**vado in ...**) and being in (**sono in ...**) for regions, counties, countries, continents and large islands):

  Vado/Sono in Lombardia/   *I'm going to/I'm in Lombardy,*
  in Cornovaglia/in Grecia/   *Cornwall, Greece,*
  in Europa/in Sicilia.   *Europe, Sicily.*

Also: in città (*in/to the town*); nel parco (*in/to the park*); in campagna (*in/to the country*); in ufficio (*in/to the office*); in montagna (*in/to the mountains*); in chiesa (*in/to church*); in vacanza (*on holiday*).

- time (seasons and centuries)
  in primavera *in spring*; in estate *in summer*; nel 1999 *in 1999*; nel secolo XXI *in the 21st century*; in anticipo/in ritardo/in orario *early/late/on time*.

In autunno iniziano le scuole. *School starts in autumn.*

With seasons you can also use **di**: d'estate (*in summer*).

- means (transport and payment)
  in autobus *by bus*; in bicicletta *by bike*; pagare in contanti *to pay cash*.

• manner:
  essere in pericolo *to be in danger*; essere in abito da sera
  to be in an evening dress; carne in umido *stewed meat*.

B Other expressions to learn: essere debole/bravo in
matematica *to be weak/good at maths*; in omaggio
complimentary (un biglietto in omaggio *a complimentary
ticket*); in apparenza *apparently*; di quando in quando *now
and again*; stare in piedi *to stand*; alzarsi in piedi *to stand up*.

Siamo in tre/quattro.   *There are three/four of us.*

Maria Schiaffino in Bianchi *Maria Bianchi neé Schiaffino*

(**In** here means *married to* since in official documents the
wife's surname is that of her father.)

exercise

Match the two halves of the sentences.

a Questa bicicletta l'ho pagata ... 1 ... una rosa in omaggio.
b Vado in ufficio in ...   2 ... di vita.
c Io prendo carne ...   3 ... in umido con patate.
d Era in pericolo ...   4 ... in contanti.
e Le signore hanno ricevuto ...   5 ... vado a trovarla.
f Di tanto in tanto ...   6 ... in piedi.
g Abbiamo dovuto viaggiare ... 7 ... autobus.

Su translates on, about, over. It combines with the definite article.

A

su +	il	lo	la	l'	i	gli	le
=	sul	sullo	sulla	sull'	sui	sugli	sulle

Su translates:

- *on, onto*

Il libro è sul tavolo.	*The book is on the table.*
La casa è costruita sulla roccia.	*The house is built on the rock.*
Firenze è sull'Arno.	*Florence is on the (river) Arno.*
La camera dà sulla spiaggia.	*The room looks onto the beach.*

- *over*

L'aereo vola su Roma.	*The plane is flying over Rome.*
Metti qualcosa sulle spalle.	*Put something over your shoulders.*

- *about, around/roughly*

una donna sulla trentina	*a woman of about 30 (years old)*
pesare sui 60 chili	*to weigh around 60 kilos*
Ha scritto un saggio sulla guerra.	*S/he wrote an essay about the war.*

B Note also these expressions:

su due piedi	*there and then*
sul momento	*at first*
fatto su misura	*made to measure*
fare sul serio	*to be in earnest*

sette su dieci	*seven out of ten*
essere sul punto di ...	*to be about to ...*
fare promesse su promesse	*to make one promise after another*
commettere errori su errori	*to make mistake after mistake*
alla televisione	*on television*

exercise

Answer the questions.

E.g. Che cosa c'è sulla rivista? → Sulla rivista c'è una penna.

a Dov'è il telefono? **b** Dov'è la penna? **c** Che c'è sul televisore? **d** Che cosa c'è scritto sulla rivista? **e** Che cosa hai visto alla televisione?

The main meaning of the preposition *per* is *for*. *Per* does not combine with the definite article.

un regalo per Maria	*a present for Maria*
per pietà	*for pity's sake*
per un mese	*for a month*
per ora	*for the present/now*
Lavori per niente?	*Do you work for nothing?*
il treno per Torino	*the train to Turin*
entrare per la finestra	*to come/go through the window*

A Per translates:

- *by* (within a period of time/means)

per il 3 maggio	*by the 3rd of May*
mandare per posta	*to send by post*

- *about* (a place)

andare in giro per la città	*to go about town*

- *on account of, out of, because of, due to, in order to*

fare qualcosa per ambizione	*to do something out of ambition*
per le condizioni del tempo	*due to the weather conditions*
per motivi di famiglia	*owing to family reasons*

- calculations, percentages

Cinque per tre fa quindici.	*Five times three is fifteen.*
dividere per cinque	*to divide by five*
il cinque per cento	*five per cent*
lo sconto del dieci per cento	*10% discount*

B Note also these expressions:

in fila per due	*two by two*

per me ...	*in my opinion ...*
per l'appunto	*exactly/precisely*
per caso	*by chance*
per di più	*moreover*
per fortuna	*luckily*
per lo più	*generally/usually/ for the most part*
per tempo	*early*
gente per bene	*honest people*
giorno per giorno	*day by day*
per modo di dire	*so to speak*
chiamare per nome	*to call by name*

exercise

Join the two columns to make meaningful sentences.

a Scusi, a che ora arriva ...   1 ... per motivi di famiglia.
b Il ladro è fuggito ...   2 ... per posta.
c Devo finire questo libro ...   3 ... per la finestra.
d Ti mando il pacco ...   4 ... per settembre.
e Va sempre in giro ...   5 ... per i boschi (*woods*).
f Credevo che lavorasse soltanto ...   6 ... il treno per Rapallo?
g È assente ...   7 ... per ambizione.
h Quanto fa ...   8 ... del cinque per cento.
i Il tasso di interesse è   9 ... sei per sei?

Tra and *fra* (*between, among, within*) are identical in meaning although one may be chosen instead of the other to avoid sounds like *tra traumi* or *fra frati*. Neither *tra* nor *fra* combines with the definite article.

> Tra il dire e il fare c'è di mezzo il mare (*proverb*).
> *Easier said than done.*

A **Tra** and **fra** translate:

* *among/between*

Detto fra/tra noi …	*Between you and me …*
Tra tutte queste auto preferisco quella rossa.	*From among all these cars I prefer the red one.*

Note the use of **quella** which here translates *the one*:
I prefer the one (which is) red.

* expressions of time

Tra un mese arriva la macchina nuova.	*In a month's time the new car will arrive.*
Tra poco esco.	*I am going out in a while.*

* place (*in the middle of*)

tra la folla	*in the middle of the crowd*

* distance (*in*)

Tra un chilometro siamo arrivati.	*In one kilometre we will be there.*

* movement towards a place (*through*)

I raggi del sole filtravano tra le persiane socchiuse.	*The sun's rays passed through the half-closed shutters.*

B Useful expressions to learn:

Ho detto fra me ...	*I said to myself ...*
tra l'altro	*besides/what is more*
Vive tra casa e ufficio.	*He lives only for work.*
Tra tutti saranno una dozzina.	*In all they must be a dozen.*
Tra i due preferisco il primo.	*Of the two I prefer the former/the first one.*
Il sole filtrava tra i rami.	*The sun filtered through the branches.*
Il ladro è scomparso tra la folla.	*The thief disappeared in the crowd.*

exercise

Join the two columns to make meaningful sentences, then read them aloud.

a Detto fra noi mi sembra che ...   1... preferisco scienze politiche.

b Tra una settimana arrivano ...   2... ci sono dieci chilometri.

c Tra il tennis e il nuoto ...   3... preferisco quest'ultimo (*the latter*).

d Tra tutte le materie (*subjects*) ...   4 ... racconti fandonie (*tall stories*).

e Ho trovato questa vecchia lettera ...   5 ... i miei amici francesi.

f Mi piace stare ...   6... tra la gente.

g Tra il dire e il fare ...   7... c'è di mezzo il mare.

h Tra casa mia e l'ufficio ...   8... siamo arrivati.

i Tra dieci chilometri ...   9... tra le pagine di un libro.

j Viale (*Avenue*) Roma è ...   10... tra due filari di pioppi (*poplars*).

The preposition *da* mainly translates *from* or *by*. It combines with the definite article.

da +	il	lo	la	l'	i	gli	le
	dal	dallo	dalla	dall'	dai	dagli	dalle

L'aereo parte da Genova.   *The plane leaves from Genoa.*
Era ammirato da tutti.   *He was admired by everyone.*
È stato assunto da loro.   *He has been employed by them.*

A Da is also used:

• to translate *to someone's place (or shop)*
Vado da Giovanni.   *I am going to Giovanni's.*
Devo andare dal farmacista.   *I must go to the chemist.*

• to translate *since* or *for*
Sono qui da ieri.   *I've been here since yesterday.*
È assente da dieci anni.   *He has been away for 10 years.*

Italian uses the present tense with the above expressions.

• to indicate value and measurements:
un francobollo da ottanta   *an 80-cent stamp*
  centesimi
una moneta da un euro   *a one euro coin*

• to indicate the purpose or use of an object
una tazza da tè   *a tea cup*
un orologio da uomo   *a man's watch*
una macchina da scrivere   *a typewriter*
una lampada da tavolo   *a table lamp*

- before an infinitive to mean *so as to, enough to*
  Fa un caldo da impazzire.   *It's hot enough to drive one mad.*
  Che cosa c'è da mangiare/   *What is there to eat/drink/see?*
    bere/vedere?

- to indicate manner (*as a/like a/worthy of*)
  Ho una fame da lupo.   *I am as hungry as a wolf.*
  un pasto da re   *a meal worthy of a king*

B Other uses:
  Fuggì/Entrò dalla porta.   *He escaped/came in through*
    the door.
  dalle mie parti   *in my part of the country*
  Ha studiato da avvocato.   *He studied to be a lawyer.*

exercise

Name the pictures and match them with the words in the box.

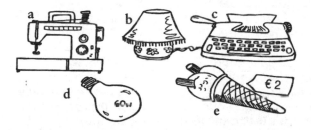

| da sessanta watts da tavolo da due euro da cucire da scrivere |

Some adjectives, adverbs and present participles can also function as prepositions. They are often, but not always, followed by *di* or *a*.

accanto a (*near*)
al posto di (*instead of*)
assieme a (*together*)
a causa di (*because of*)
a dispetto di (*despite*)
ad eccezione di (*except for*)
a seconda di (*according to*)
attraverso (*through/across*)
circa (*about*)
contro* (*against*)
davanti a (*in front of*)
dentro* (*inside*)
dietro* (*behind*)
di fronte a (*opposite*)
dopo* (*after*)
durante (*during*)
eccetto (*except*)
fino a (*as far as/until*)
fuori di (*outside/out of*)
in cima a (*at the top of*)
in fondo a (*at the bottom of*)
in mezzo a (*in the middle of*)
insieme con (*together with*)

intorno a (*around*)
invece di (*instead of*)
lontano da (*far from*)
lungo (*along*)
malgrado (*in spite of*)
nel mezzo di (*in the middle of*)
nonostante (*notwithstanding*)
per mezzo di (*by means of/through*)
prima di (*before*)
presso* (*near/not far from*)
riguardo a (*regarding*)
rispetto a (*with respect to/as to*)
salvo (*except for*)
secondo (*according to*)
senza* (*without*)
sino a (*as far as/until*)
sopra* (*above*)
sotto* (*under/beneath*)
tramite (*by means of/through*)
tranne (*except for*)
verso* (*towards*)
vicino a (*near/next to*)

The prepositions marked * take **di** when followed by **me, te, lui, lei, noi, voi** or **loro**.

exercise

Complete the sentences using the prepositions in the box.

a L'automobile è _____ .
b Gli alberi sono _____ .
c La collina è _____ .
d La bicicletta è _____ .

| davanti a | dietro | in cima a | vicino a |

Translate the following into Italian.

e The car stopped in the middle of the road.
f They were all present except for two.
g I couldn't hear because of the noise (**rumore**).
h Is Lucca far from here?
i The fountain is next to the Basilica.
j Today the pound is up (**in rialzo**) with respect to the dollar (**dollaro**).

Adverbs can also modify adjectives and other adverbs as well as verbs.

A In English, most adverbs are formed by adding *-ly* to the adjective: *slow* (adjective) becomes *slowly* (adverb). In Italian, **-mente** is added to the feminine form of the adjective: **lenta** (adjective) becomes **lentamente** (adverb).

- Adjectives ending in -e just add -mente: **veloce** → **velocemente**.
- Adverbs are usually placed next to the verb they modify.
  Lavora intensamente.   *He works constantly.*
- Most adjectives ending in -le and -re drop their final vowel before adding -mente: **facile** → **facilmente**, **regolare** → **regolarmente**.

B As well as a verb, adverbs can modify an adjective or another adverb.

Siamo molto lieti di   *We are pleased to make*
conoscerLa.   *your acquaintance.*

In this example, **molto** is the adverb modifying the adjective **lieti**.

Il professore ha spiegato la   *The teacher has explained the*
lezione molto chiaramente.   *lesson very clearly.*

In the above example, the adverb **molto** qualifies the adverb **chiaramente**.

C Adverbs are invariable, so remember that when **molto**, **tanto** or **troppo** are used as adverbs, they remain as they are, whereas when used as adjectives they agree with the noun.

molto bella *very beautiful*   molte telefonate *many telephone calls*

D Other adjectives which can be used as adverbs are: **vicino** (*nearby*); **lontano** (*far away*); **chiaro/chiaramente** (*clearly*); **forte** (*loudly*); **duro** (*hard*); **solo** or **soltanto/solamente** (*only*): Parla troppo forte. *He speaks too loudly.*

E In English, *better* and *worse* can be either adjectives or adverbs. In Italian, they have two different forms as follows:

| adverbs | bene (*well*) meglio (*better*) | male (*badly*) peggio (*worse*) |
| adjectives | buono (*good*) migliore (*better*) | cattivo (*bad*) peggiore (*worse*) |

Parla italiano molto bene.   *S/he speaks Italian very well.*
Va di bene in meglio.   *It's getting better and better.*

exercise

Form the adverb from the following adjectives.

a chiaro	g magnifico	m forte
b cattivo	h inutile	n duro
c veloce	i probabile	o elegante
d difficile	j agile	p ovvio
e grande	k gentile	q cortese
f rapido	l maggiore	r molle

While many Italian adverbs derive from adjectives, others have a different form.

A Adverbs of manner express the way in which something happens. These include most of those ending in **-mente** dealt with in the previous unit.

B Adverbs of time include: ora/adesso (*now*); allora (*then/at that time*); ancora (*still/yet/again*); annualmente (*yearly*); appena (*just/scarcely/hardly*); domani (*tomorrow*); dopo (*afterwards*); dopodomani (*the day after tomorrow*); finora (*until now*); già (*already*); ieri (*yesterday*); mai (*never*); mensilmente (*monthly*); oggi (*today*); ormai (*by now/by then*); poi (*next/then*); presto (*soon/quickly*); raramente (*seldom*); sempre (*always*); settimanalmente (*weekly*); spesso (*often*); subito (*immediately/at once*); tardi (*late*).

Adverbial expressions of time: per tempo (*early*), per ora (*for the time being*), di quando in quando (*every so often*).

C Adverbs of place include: altrove (*somewhere else*); davanti (*in front*); dappertutto (*everywhere*); dentro (*inside*); dietro (*behind*); fuori (*outside*); laggiù (*over/down there*); lassù (*up there*); lì/là (*there*); lontano (*far away*); oltre (*farther/further*); qui/qua (*here*); quaggiù (*down here*); quassù (*up here*); sopra/su (*up*); sotto (*underneath*); vicino (*nearby*).

Adverbial expressions of place include: di sopra (*upstairs*); di sotto (*downstairs*); in su (*upwards*); in giù (*downwards*); per di qua (*this way*); per di là (*that way*).

D Adverbs of quantity include: abbastanza (*sufficiently/enough*); parecchio/alquanto (*quite/rather*); altrettanto (*equally*); assai (*a lot/much*); meno (*less*); molto (*a lot/(very) much/a great deal*); niente/nulla (*not at all*); poco (*little*); quanto (*how much/how far*).

Adverbial expressions of quantity include: pressapoco/all'incirca (*approximately*); né più né meno (*no more no less*).

E Other adverbs or adverbial expressions: certo/certamente/sicuro/sicuramente (*certainly/of course/sure*); appunto (*exactly*); nemmeno/neanche, neppure (*not even*); non (*not*); forse (*perhaps*); quasi (*almost*); eventualmente (*if needs be/if necessary*); probabilmente (*probably*); da lontano (*from a distance*); da vicino (*closely*); in generale (*in general*); in breve (*in short*); di solito (*usually*).

exercise

Match the two halves of the sentences.

a Pago il lattaio ...
b Ricevo lo stipendio ...
c Pago le tasse ...
d Ieri stavo male ...
e Ormai ...
f Vado spesso ...
g Vieni qui ...

1 ... in discoteca.
2 ... ma oggi sto bene.
3 ... è troppo tardi.
4 ... mensilmente.
5 ... annualmente.
6 ... settimanalmente.
7 ... immediatamente.

There is not always a strict rule as to where the adverb should go. However, there are some rules that do need to be followed.

A With many adverbs, of manner in particular, the position of the adverb is free, its position only slightly changing the emphasis of its meaning.

Generalmente esco la domenica.
Esco generalmente la domenica. } *I usually go out on Sundays.*
La domenica esco, generalmente.

B Generally the adverb goes before the adjective or another adverb, as in English.

Questa casa è troppo rumorosa. *This house is too noisy.*

C When an adverb qualifies a verb, it usually goes after it …

Abitano lontano. *They live far away.*
Io mi siedo davanti. *I sit in front.*

… but **ieri, oggi** and **domani** tend to be placed before the verb.

Domani scade l'abbonamento alla TV. *The TV licence is due tomorrow.*

Ieri ha fatto bel tempo. *The weather was fine yesterday.*

D With compound tenses, the adverbs of time **ancora, appena, già, mai** and **sempre** are placed, as in English, between the auxiliary and the verb.

Sono sempre andata in vacanza al mare. *I have always been on holiday to the seaside.*

Marco è già partito.   *Marco has already left.*
Quel film l'ho già visto.   *I have already seen that film.*
Non ho ancora finito.   *I have not finished yet.*

exercises

1 Choose a suitable adverb from the box for each sentence and add it in the correct place.

a È una persona che si emoziona …
b D'estate piove …
c Parla italiano …
d Se vuoi farti capire devi parlare …
e Ha continuato a negare …
f Vedo che hai studiato …
g Non ho finito …

> chiaramente
> diligentemente
> raramente
> correntemente
> facilmente
> fermamente
> ancora

2 Put the words in the right order.

a onestamente lavorato sempre Ha
b alla domanda mia debolmente Rispose
c letto già Ho libro quel
d ricco Non molto interiormente è

3 Each number corresponds to the same letter each time it is used. With the help of the clues, find the adverbs.

a 12 2 8 4 5 4 6 7 3 9 10 11 9
  quasi certamente
b 12 8 13 13 6 4 6 7 3 9 10 11 9
  per quanto possibile
c 7 8 10 11 5 10 8
  non vicino

Conjunctions do not change their form. They join two words to make a phrase, or two phrases (or clauses) to make a longer, more complex sentence.

A Some conjunctions join two words or two separate phrases which otherwise could stand by themselves: *This book is expensive + This book is interesting = This book is expensive but/and interesting*.

B Among the most common conjunctions are:

- **anche** (*also/too*)
  È venuta anche Mariangela. *Mariangela came too.*

- **e** (*and*); to sound better e acquires a -d before a vowel – particularly before another **e**:
  Ho visto Carla ed Enrica.   *I saw Carla and Enrica.*

- **eppure/tuttavia** (*yet/nevertheless*)
  Tu non mi credi, eppure   *You don't believe me, and yet*
  è vero.   *it is true.*

- **anzi** (*on the contrary*)
  Oggi non fa freddo, anzi, fa   *Today isn't cold, on the*
  piuttosto caldo.   *contrary it's rather warm.*

- **quindi/dunque/perciò** (*so/therefore*)
  È tardi perciò vado.   *It's late so I'll go.*

- **ma/però** (*but*)
  È caro ma/però è buono.   *It's expensive but good.*

- **siccome/poiché** (*since/as*)
  Siccome era tardi sono   *Since it was late I returned*
  tornato a casa.   *home.*

- **mentre** (*while/whilst*)

  È venuto mentre ero fuori.   *He came while I was out.*

- **cioè** (*that is (to say)/namely*)

  Sarò lì alle cinque cioè tra   *I'll be there at five, that is*
  due ore.   *in two hours' time.*

- **infatti** (*in fact*)

  Mi sembrava troppo caro,   *I thought it was too*
  infatti c'era un errore   *expensive; in fact there was*
  nel conto.   *a mistake on the bill.*

- **o/oppure** (*or*); **o … o/oppure** (*either … or*)

  Vuoi questo o quello?   *Do you want this one or*
                           that one?

  o questo o quello   *either this one or that one*

- **sia … sia/sia … che** (*both … and*)

  Ho comprato sia la cassetta   *I bought both the cassette*
  che il CD.   *and the CD.*

- **né … né** (*neither … nor*)

  né carne né pesce   *neither fish nor fowl*

- **non solo/soltanto … ma** (*not only … but*)

  È un libro non soltanto   *It's not only an amusing*
  divertente ma anche   *book but also educational.*
  istruttivo.

- **se** (*if*)

  Se fossi in te   *If I were you*

exercise

See Exercise 67 in the 'More practice' section.

Below is a list of conjunctions joining two phrases together, one of which is subordinate to the other.

In the phrase *I study Italian because I want to speak and understand it*, the first part (*I study Italian*) can stand by itself, this is the main clause; the second (*because I want …*) is the dependent clause. Below is a list of conjunctions introducing a dependent clause which requires a subjunctive.

- **a condizione che/a patto che** *(on condition (that))*
  Vengo a condizione che venga anche lui.
  I'll go on condition that he (comes) goes too.

- **purché** *(as long as)*
  Ti aiuto purché tu non lo dica a Maria.
  I'll help you as long as you do not tell Maria.

- **anche se** *(even if)*
  Uscirebbe anche se grandinasse.
  S/he would go out even if it was hailing.

- **qualora** *(in case/if)*
  Qualora me ne dimenticassi, ti prego di ricordarmelo.
  In case I forget, please remind me.

- **che** *(that)*
  Penso che sia uscito.
  I think he has gone out.

- **benché/nonostante/sebbene** *(although/notwithstanding/even though)*
  Benché fosse in ritardo, se la prese con comodo.
  Even though she was late, she took it easy.
  Sebbene abbia perso tutto, è sempre molto allegro.
  Although he lost everything, he is always cheerful.

- **a meno che (non)** (*unless*) (See Unit 89, 'False negatives'.)
  Non supererai l'esame a   *You will not pass the exam*
    meno che non studi di più.   *unless you study more.*
- **prima che** (*before*)
  Pensaci prima che sia   *Think about it before it is*
    troppo tardi.   *too late.*
- **affinché/in modo che** (*so that/in order that*)
  Protesto affinché sia fatta   *I protest in order that justice*
    giustizia.   *be done.*

As you can see from many of the examples above, the
dependent clause can be placed at the beginning of the sentence.

exercise

Match the two halves of the sentences.

a Ti do la macchina a patto che…   1… prima che perda
     la pazienza.

b Ti permetto di andare in discoteca …   2… a meno che non piova.

c Rimarrebbe calmo anche se …   3… non ho ricevuto
     la lettera.

d Nel caso che io non ritornassi in
    tempo …   4… sono stato bocciato.

e So che lui …   5… è una persona onesta.

f Nonostante abbia studiato …   6… fai tu la spesa.

g Sebbene lui mi abbia scritto …   7… cascasse il mondo.

h Domani pianterò i fiori in giardino …   8… tu compri la benzina.

i Vai via …   9… purché ritorni per
     mezzanotte.

An interjection is a part of speech that doesn't change and is used to express a mood or to call someone's attention.

A Among the most common interjections are: ah! oh! eh! uh! ih!, the meaning of which depends mainly on the tone of one's voice.

B Others, not depending on the tone of the voice, are:
- auff! uff! uffa! (*to show impatience*) Uffa, che noia! *How boring!*
- ehi!/ehilà! (*hey! hullo! you there! ahoy!*)
- ohi! ohé! (*to call someone*)
- mah! (*who knows!*) (to show uncertainty, doubt or resignation; the latter often accompanied by a very slight shake of one's head)
- ahimè!/ohimé (*alas!*)
- puh! puah! (*to show repulsion*)

C Interjections are usually followed by an exclamation mark which can appear at the end of the sentence, in which case the interjection is followed by a comma: Ehi, sto parlando a te! *Hey I am talking to you!*

D Some other expressions used as exclamations are:

Alla buon'ora! (*At last! Finally!*) Vallo a raccontare ad un altro!
Mamma mia! (*Dear me!*)   (*Tell that to the marines!*)
Santo cielo! (*Goodness gracious!*) Meno male! (*Thank goodness!*)
Bravo! Brava! (*Well done!*)   Che bugiardo! (*What a fibber!*)
Evviva! Viva! (*Hurray! hurrah!*)Che stupido! (*How stupid!*)
Salve! (*Hello!*)   Che coraggio! (*How brave!*)

Bene! (*Well! All right! OK!*)   Accidenti! (*My goodness!/Damn it!*)
Sicuro! (*Of course! Sure!*)   Povero me! (*Poor me!*)
Su!/Dai! (*Come on! Come (now)!*)   Coraggio! (*Take heart!*)
Che fregatura! (*What a rip-off*)!   Che barba! (*How boring!*)
Per carità! (*For pity's sake!/please!*)
Per amor del cielo! (*For heaven's sake!*)
Via! (*Go away!/(to start a race or similar) Go!/ (to incite)
Come on!*)

exercise

**Choose one of the expressions in the box in response to each
sentence of your friend's account of his holiday in Kenya.**

> Dai, vallo a raccontare ad un altro! Che coraggio! Che stupido!
> Accidenti che sfortuna! Che bugiardo che sei! Meno male!

a Quando ero in Kenia ho noleggiato una jeep e sono andato
a fare un safari da solo …
b Ad un certo punto ho visto un leone, allora ho fermato la
macchina e sono sceso.
c Avevo lasciato la portiera aperta nel caso che il leone mi
attaccasse …
d Soltanto che una folata di vento ha chiuso la portiera.
e Pensa che io ero completamente solo e disarmato ma mi è
bastato schioccare le dita per farlo fuggire!
f Non mi credi? Eppure ti assicuro che è vero.

The negative form is made by placing *non* before the verb.

A A pronoun cannot be separated from the verb, so **non** in this case precedes the pronoun.

Ti è piaciuto il film?	*Did you like the film?*
No, non mi è piaciuto.	*No, I didn't like it.*

Remember that **no** (*no*) isn't a substitute for **non** (*not*).

B Negative words or expressions such as **niente/nulla** (*nothing*), **nessuno** (*none/nobody*), **in nessun luogo/da nessuna parte** (*nowhere*), **mai** (*never*), **per niente** (*at all*), are used together with **non**.

Non c'è nessuno.	*There is nobody.*
Non lo trovo da nessuna parte.	*I cannot see it anywhere.*
Non viene mai nessuno.	*Nobody ever comes.*

When a negative word is used as a subject, **non** is omitted.

Nessuno sa chi sia.	*Nobody knows who he is.*
Niente può fermarlo.	*He stops at nothing.*

C Negative expressions

- **non ... mai** (*never, not ever*)
  Non lo vedo mai.   *I never see him.*
- **non ... nessuno** (*not ... anybody, nobody*)
  Non vedo nessuno.   *I don't see anybody.*
- **non ... mai nessuno** (*never ... anybody*)
  Non vedo mai nessuno.   *I never see anybody.*
- **non ... niente/nulla** (*nothing/not anything*)
  Non vedo nulla.   *I can't see anything.*
- **non ... mai niente** (*never ... anything*)
  Non dice mai niente.   *He never says anything.*

- **non ... per niente/affatto** (*not ... at all*)
  Non mi piace per niente.   *I don't like it at all.*
- **non ... neanche/neppure/nemmeno** (*not ... even*)
  Non l'ha neppure ringraziato. *She didn't even thank him.*
- **non ... più** (*no more/no longer/not any more*)
  Non dipingo più.   *I no longer paint.*
- **non ... da nessuna parte** (*not ... anywhere, nowhere*)
  Carla non va da nessuna parte. *Carla doesn't go anywhere.*
- **non ... né ... né** (*neither ... nor*)
  Non voglio né l'uno né l'altro. *I want neither the one nor the other.*

exercise

Change these sentences to mean the opposite.

E.g. Compro sempre il giornale. → Non compro mai il giornale.
Mi piacciono tutti e due. → Non mi piace né l'uno né l'altro.
Vai ancora in vacanza a Lucca? → No, non ci vado più.

a C'era molta gente.
b C'è sempre molta gente.
c Ha molto da fare.
d Ha sempre molto da fare.

e Sa tutto.
f Sa sempre tutto.
g Mi piace moltissimo.
h Mi ha ringraziato.

Answer the questions in the negative.

E.g. Vi è piaciuta la commedia? → No, non ci è piaciuta.
Scrivi spesso a Marianna? → No, non le scrivo mai.

i Ti sono piaciuti i film?
j Vi è piaciuto lo spettacolo?
k Lo vedi spesso?

l C'era qualcuno nel parco?
m Hai qualcosa per me?
n Giochi ancora (*still*) a tennis?

There are some expressions using *non* which are not negative. There are also some prefixes which give words a negative value.

A Positive expressions containing **non**:

- **a meno che non** (*unless*) (requires the subjunctive)

Arriverò alle tre a meno	*I will arrive by three o'clock*
che non ci sia troppo traffico.	*unless there is too much traffic.*

- **finché non** (*until/till*)

Non potrò uscire finché non	*I will not be able to go out*
avrò finito questo.	*until I have finished this.*

- **non + verb + che** (*only/nothing but*)

Non possiamo che attendere i	*We can only wait for the*
risultati degli esami.	*exam results./We can do nothing but wait for the exam results.*

B As in English, some letters added at the beginning of a word (a prefix) may change the meaning of it.

- The prefix **ri-**, similar to the English **re-**, is often used in the sense of *again*: elaborare (*to elaborate*), rielaborare (*to elaborate/work out again*); vedere (*to see*), rivedere (*to see/meet again*); formare (*to form*), riformare (*to re-form/shape again*); provare (*to try*), riprovare (*to try again*).

- The prefix **s-** often (but not always) gives adjectives, verbs and nouns an opposite meaning:
  fiorire (*to bloom*), sfiorire (*to wither*); fiducia (*trust*), sfiducia (*mistrust/distrust*); legare (*to tie/fasten*), slegare (*to untie*); proporzionato (*proportional/proportionate*),

sproporzionato (*disproportional*).

- The prefix **in-** gives a 'not' value and is used mainly before adjectives and nouns:
  abile (*able/capable*), inabile (*unable/incapable*); fedeltà (*fidelity/faithfulness*), infedeltà (*infidelity/unfaithfulness*).
- The prefixes **de-**, **di-** and **dis-**, also have a negative value:
  centralizzare (*to centralize*), decentralizzare/decentrare (*to decentralize*); sperare (*to hope*), disperare (*to despair*); armare (*to arm*), disarmare (*to disarm*).
- **contro**, **contra** express opposition:
  indicato (*suitable/apt/advisable*), controindicato (*inadvisable*); dire (*to say*), contraddire (*to contradict*).

exercise

Choose between *finché non* … or *a meno che non* … and complete the sentences below.

a Ti aspetterò _____ arriverai.
b Ti scriverò _____ sia troppo occupata.
c Non lo sapevo _____ me lo hai detto tu.
d Lo seguì con lo sguardo _____ lo vide scomparire dietro l'angolo.
e Lo comprerò _____ sia troppo caro.

Give the opposite meaning to the following sentences by adding or deleting the prefixes *s-*, *in-*, *de-*, *contro*, etc. as necessary.

f Questa medicina è indicata per i sofferenti di cuore.
g Quel macchinario è in uso dall'anno scorso.
h Dispero di riuscire.
i Il governo ha deciso di centralizzare i servizi pubblici.

Who, whom, which, that, he who, etc. are called **relative pronouns**. In Italian, *che* is mostly used except for a few cases explained below.

> che = who, whom, which, that
> di, a, da, etc. + cui = of, to, from, etc. whom/which
> il, la, i, le + cui = whose

A **Che** doesn't change and is used both as a subject and an object.

l'attore che ha recitato Amleto	*the actor who played Hamlet*
l'attrice che ti ho presentato	*the actress (whom) I introduced to you*
il fax che ti ho spedito	*the fax (that) I sent you*

Il/la quale, i/le quali can be used instead of **che** to avoid ambiguity:

È il figlio della mia vicina che ha scritto da Cambridge.
He is the son of my neighbour who wrote from Cambridge.
(*Who wrote?*) È il figlio della mia vicina la quale ha scritto da Cambridge. (*la vicina*) È il figlio della mia vicina il quale ha scritto da Cambridge. (*il figlio*)

Unlike English, the relative pronoun MUST NOT be omitted.

B **Cui** is invariable and is used instead of **che** after a preposition.

la città da cui vengo	*the town from which I come*
il ragazzo con cui esco	*the boy I go out with (with whom I go out)*
la nave in cui ho viaggiato	*the ship in which I travelled*

C Il/la/i/le cui + noun translate *whose* + noun:

La cliente il cui fax è arrivato
ieri è al telefono.

*The client whose fax arrived
yesterday is on the phone.*

Il libro, il cui autore è mio
amico, è arrivato questa
mattina.

*The book, whose author is a
friend of mine, has arrived
this morning.*

Whose can also be translated by **il/lo/la/l'/i/gli/le** + noun +
del/della quale, dei/delle quali.

La cliente il fax della quale è arrivato questa mattina è al telefono.

Il libro, l'autore del quale è mio amico, è arrivato questa mattina.

exercises

Match the two halves of the sentences, then read them aloud.

a la lettera che ...

b l'autobus ...

c gli studenti che...

d il programma che ...

e il pittore che ti ha ...

f l'attrice che ha ...

g i soldi che ...

h l'amico ...

1 ... ti ho prestato

2 ... recitato 'Fedora'

3 ... ho visto alla TV

4 ... che ho preso

5 ... ti ho scritto

6 ... fatto il ritratto

7 ... che ti ho presentato

8 ... hanno superato l'esame

Add *di*, *a*, *da*, etc. + *cui* to the sentences below.

i La cittadina _____ viene si chiama Viareggio.

j La poltrona _____ siedo è molto comoda.

k La ragione _____ non ti scrivo è che non ho molto tempo.

l L'autobus _____ vado in ufficio è il numero 39.

m La persona _____ ho chiesto un'informazione era straniera.

English uses *what* as an interrogative pronoun (*What is this?*) as well as a relative pronoun (*what you say is right*). Italian uses two different words.

ciò che/quello che = what	colui che = he who
tutto ciò che/tutto quello che = all that	colei che = she who
chi = he/she/those who	coloro che = those who

A Ciò che and quello che have the same meaning.

Ciò che dici è molto interessante.	*What you say is very interesting.*
Quello che fai è affar tuo.	*What you do is your business.*

B Chi doesn't change and can only refer to people. It is used in the singular even when referring to more than one person. It can be substituted by colui che (masculine), colei che (feminine) or coloro che (masculine and feminine plural).

Chi è interessato scriva al seguente indirizzo.	
Coloro che sono interessati scrivano al seguente indirizzo.	*Whoever is interested must write to the following address.*

Chi is also used in proverbs.

Chi vuole vada, chi non vuole mandi.	*If you want a thing done, go; if not send someone.*
Chi s'aiuta, Dio l'aiuta.	*God helps those who help themselves.*
Chi vivrà, vedrà.	*Time will tell.*

C **Tutto ciò che** and **tutto quello che** have the same meaning.

Questo è tutto quello che so. *This is all I know.*

Di tutto ciò che ha scritto gli *Of all he wrote only one*
hanno pubblicato soltanto *book was published.*
un libro.

exercise

Translate the following into Italian.

a We bought all (that) we could.
b What she does is not my concern.
c What counts is to be healthy.
d What they say is false.
e They gave her all (that) they had.
f Is this all you (*tu*) can do?
g This is all I know.
h They took all there was.

92 indefinite pronouns

These words stand in place of nouns. They are called indefinite because the exact number of persons or objects they represent is not specified.

A Common indefinite pronouns

• **chiunque** (*anybody/anyone/whoever*)

Chiunque venga digli di attendere.	*Whoever comes tell him to wait.*

• **qualunque/qualsiasi**

qualunque cosa	*anything*
a qualunque/qualsiasi costo	*at any cost*

• **niente/nulla** (*nothing, anything*)

Non si accorge mai di nulla.	*She never notices anything.*

• **ognuno** (*everybody/everyone/each one*)

Ognuno ha donato dieci sterline.	*Each one gave ten pounds.*

• **qualcosa/qualche cosa** (*something, anything*)

Vuoi qualcosa da bere?	*Would you like something to drink?*

• **qualcuno** (*someone/somebody, anybody/anyone, some*)

C'è qualcuno che ti vuole.	*There is someone asking for you.*
Ne prendo qualcuna.	*I'll take some (f.).*

Qualcuno becomes **qualcun** before **altro** and **qualcun'** before **altra**.

Verrà qualcun altro.	*Someone else will come.*

• **uno** (*one/someone/somebody/each*)

uno di noi	*one of us*
Costano un euro l'una.	*They cost one euro each.*

Ognuno, qualcuno and **uno** have feminine forms; all the others are invariable.

B These indefinite words can function both as pronouns and adjectives.

- **alcun, alcuno (-a,-i,-e)** *(some* (usually plural))
- **ciascun, ciascuno, ciascuna** *(everybody/each (one))*
- **nessun, nessuno, nessuna, nessun'** *(nobody/no one/none/no)*
- **altro (-a,-i,-e)** *(another (one)/other)*
- **parecchio (-a,-i,-e)** *(several/quite a few/a lot of/lots of)*
- **molto/tanto (-a,-i,-e)** *(much/a lot)*
- **troppo (-a,-i,-e)** *(too much/too many)*
- **poco (poca, pochi, poche)** *(a little/a few)*
- **tutto (-a,-i,-e)** *(all/everything/everybody)*

exercise

Choose the correct word from the box to complete the sentences.

a Non vedo _____ .
b Non voglio _____ .
c _____ aveva qualcosa da dire.
d Vorrei _____ di più elegante.
e C'è _____ che vuole una fetta di torta?
f Chiedilo a _____ altro.
g È _____ del nostro gruppo.
h _____ sia digli di attendere.

| chiunque |
| niente |
| nessuno |
| ciascuno |
| qualcun |
| uno |
| qualcuno |
| qualcosa |

Interrogative words are usually placed at the beginning of a sentence. This and the next two units will show examples of their use.

| Chi? | *Who?* | Quale? | *Which (one)? What?* |
| Che (cosa)? | *What?* | | |

A **Chi?** is invariable and is used only for people.

| Chi è venuto alla festa? | *Who came to the party?* |
| Chi è? | *Who is it?* |

B **Che (cosa)?** doesn't change and is used for things. You may ask either **Che ... ?** or **Che cosa ... ?** (lit.: *What thing?*). Nowadays many people just say **Cosa ... ?**.

Che vuoi?
Che cosa vuoi?   *What do you want?*
Cosa vuoi?

C **Quale?** has a plural form (**quali?**).

| Quale preferisci? | *Which one do you want?* |
| Quali vuoi? | *Which ones do you want?* |

Quale becomes **qual** before è and era.

| Qual è la tua opinione? | *What is your opinion?* |

The difference between **quale** and **che** is that the former implies a choice between two or more options.

| Qual è la tua auto? | *Which (one) is your car?* |
| Che auto hai? | *What car do you have?* |

exercises

1 Complete the sentences with *chi?*, *che (cosa)?*, or *quale(-i)?*

a _____ c'era alla festa?

b _____ viene con me al cinema?

c _____ sigarette preferisci?

d _____ hai nella borsa?

e _____ c'è in questa scatola?

f _____ vuoi per cena?

g _____ è la tua decisione?

h _____ hai deciso?

i _____ tavolo vuole?

j _____ ha mangiato la mia torta?

k _____ sceglieresti?

2 Form questions by joining phrases from the two columns as appropriate and then read them aloud.

a Chi hai visto ...

b Che cosa c'è ...

c Che ...

d Che cosa pensi ...

e Che cosa vai ...

f Chi ha ...

g Chi è ...

1... quell'uomo?

2... parlato?

3... di fare?

4... alla festa?

5... per cena?

6... vuoi?

7... a fare?

3 Translate into Italian.

a Which is your husband?

b What is your job?

c Who went to the party?

d What did you see?

e Which is your coat?

f What do they want?

Other common Italian interrogative words are: *Come?* (How?), *Quando?* (When?), *Quanto (-a, -i, -e)?* (How much/many?) and *Perché?* (Why?).

A Come? *(How?)*

Come stai?	*How are you?*
Come ti chiami?	*What's your name? (lit. How do you call yourself?)*
Come?/Come hai detto?	*Pardon?/What did you say?*
Com'è il tuo ragazzo?	*What is your boyfriend like?*
Com'è che...?/Come mai*...?	*How come?/Why on earth?*

*mai *(never/ever)* is often used to emphasize an adverb.

B Quando? *(When?)*

Quando parte?	*When does it leave?*
Da quando?	*Since when?*
Da quando sei qui?	*How long have you been here?*
Di quando è questo giornale?	*Which day's paper is this?*
Per quando lo vuole?	*When do you want it for?*

C Quanto/-a/-i/-e? *(How much/many?* With time: *How long...?)*

Quanti soldi hai?	*How much money do you have?*
Quanti anni hai?	*How old are you? (lit.: How many years do you have?)*
Quanto (tempo)?	*How long?/How much time?*
Quanto (tempo) ci vuole?	*How long does it take?*
Quanto (tempo) ci mette il battello?	*How long does the boat take?*

Quante volte? Ogni quanto?	*How many times?/How often?*
Quanti ne abbiamo oggi?	*What is the date today?*
Quant'è?	*How much is it?*
Da quanto lo vuole?	*Of what value do you want it?*
Da quanto tempo?	*Since when?*
Quanto è alto (lungo/ largo/spesso/grande)?	*How tall/high (long/ wide/thick/large) is it?*
Quanto dista?	*How far is it?*

D Perché? *(Why?)*

Perché non glielo chiedi?	*Why don't you ask him?*
Perché no?	*Why not?*
Perché mai …?	*Why on earth …?*

exercise

Match the two halves to form questions.

a Come …	1 … ore ci vogliono per andare a Fiesole?
b Quante …	2 … è questo pane?
c Perché mai …	3 … dovrò attendere?
d Quanti …	4 … è entrata in vigore la legge (*the law was enforced*)?
e Per quando …	5 … ne ha bisogno?
f Fino a quando …	6 … sei così in ritardo?
g Di quando …	7 … chilometri ci sono da qui a Soli?
h Da quando…	8 … dice?

More interrogative words: *Dove?* (Where?), *A che ora?* (At what time?), *Di chi è?* (Whose is it?), *Che tipo?* (What kind?).

A Dove? *(Where?)*

Dove sono i miei occhiali?	*Where are my glasses?*
Dov'è il museo?	*Where is the museum?*
Da dove viene?	*Where do you come from?*
Di dov'è Lei, Signora?	*Where are you from, madam?*
Il treno per dove?	*The train going where?*

B A che ora? *(At what time?)*

A che ora è la colazione?	*What time is breakfast?*
A che ora comincia la festa?	*At what time does the party start?*

Che ora è?/Che ore sono? *(What time is it?)*

Scusi, sa che ore sono?	*Excuse me, do you know the time?*

C Di chi? *(Whose?)*

Di chi sono queste carte?	*Whose papers are these?*
Di chi è quel quadro?	*Whose painting is that?*

D Che tipo? *(What kind?)*

Che tipo di sciampo desidera?	*What kind of shampoo do you want?*
Che tipi ha?	*What kinds do you have?*
Che tipo è il tuo principale?	*What kind of person is your boss?*

E Other interrogative expressions

Che cosa succede?	*What's going on?*
Che cosa ti/Le/vi succede?	*What is the matter with you?*

Che cosa danno al cinema?	*What's on at the cinema?*
A chi tocca?	*Whose turn is it?*
A che scopo?/ (E) perché?	*What for?*
E con ciò?	*So what?*

exercises

Match the questions and the answers.

a	E perché?	1	Un'utilitaria che costi poco.
b	E con ciò?	2	Mie.
c	A chi tocca?	3	Perché non rispondi educatamente?
d	Che cosa danno al cinema?	4	Perché sì!
e	Che cos'hai?	5	Una commedia brillante.
f	Che cosa succede?	6	Non mi sento bene.
g	Che tipo di auto ha in mente?	7	Niente. Perché?
h	Di chi sono queste valigie?	8	A me.
i	L'autobus per dove?	9	Lucca.

Write the questions for these answers.

j	A me.	o	Perché te lo dico io!
k	Un film di cowboys.	p	Vengo da Padova.
l	Mi sento male.	q	È sotto il tavolo.
m	Ne ho di molti tipi.	r	Comincia alle tre.
n	Ho un cesto (*basket*) di ciliege.	s	È mio.

96 'false friends'

There are many Italian words that, despite being very similar to English words, have a different meaning. Below is a list of the most common ones.

ITALIAN – ENGLISH	ENGLISH – ITALIAN
annoiare (*to bore*)	*to annoy* (infastidire)
anticipare (*to be early*)	*to anticipate* (prevedere)
argomento (*topic*)	*argument* (disputa)
atteggiamento (*attitude*)	*aptitude* (attitudine)
attendere (*to wait for*)	*to attend* (frequentare)
attuale (*current*)	*actual* (reale/vero/concreto)
attualmente (*at present*)	*actually* (veramente/in verità)
avvisare (*to warn*)	*to advise* (consigliare)
camera (*room*)	*camera* (macchina fotografica)
cantina (*cellar*)	*canteen* (mensa)
coincidenza (*(transport) connection*)	*coincidence* (coincidenza)
confetti (*sugared almonds*)	*confetti* (coriandoli)
confezione (*wrapping of a product/ ready-to-wear clothes*)	*confectionery* (dolciumi)
conveniente (*advantageous/cheap*)	*convenient* (comodo)
costipazione (*a bad cold*)	*constipation* (stitichezza)
educato (*well-mannered*)	*educated* (istruito)
facilità (*easiness/ease*)	*facilities* (attrezzature)
fattoria (*farm*)	*factory* (fabbrica)
firma (*signature*)	*firm* (ditta/società/compagnia)
grave (*serious/severe*)	*grave* (tomba)
incidente (*accident*)	*incident* (avvenimento/episodio)
intossicazione (*food poisoning*)	*intoxication* (ubriachezza)

libreria (*bookshop*)	*library* (biblioteca)
magazzino (*warehouse/department store*)	*magazine* (rivista)
marmellata (*jam*)	*marmalade* (marmellata d'arancia)
morbido (*soft*)	*morbid* (morboso)
parenti (*relatives*)	*parents* (genitori)
patente (*driving licence*)	*patent* (brevetto)
pavimento (*floor*)	*pavement* (marciapiede)
petrolio (*crude oil*)	*petrol* (benzina)
preventivo (*estimate*)	*prevention* (prevenzione)
sensibile (*sensitive*)	*sensible* (saggio/sensato)

exercise

Match the two halves of the sentences.

a Ti aspetto sul marciapiede…
b Il malato è grave, …
c Io prendo pane tostato con …
d È un golfino molto morbido: …
e Vorrei un preventivo …
f Attualmente …
g Devo andare in biblioteca …
h Devo andare in libreria …
i Veramente avrei preferito …
j Ha sempre un atteggiamento …

1 … è di cachemire.
2 … per la riparazione del tetto.
3 … vivo a Brighton.
4 … accanto al Duomo.
5 … non bisogna disturbarlo.
6 … marmellata d'arancia.
7 … non occuparmi della
     faccenda.
8 … da superuomo.
9 … a comprare un libro.
10 … a consultare un libro.

Unit 1: a Maria mangia una banana. **b** Paolo mangia una pizza perché ha fame.

Unit 2: a Posso andare? Non posso andare. **b** Posso parlare? Non posso parlare. **c** Devo pagare il conto? Non devo pagare il conto. **d** Devo scrivere la lettera? Non devo scrivere la lettera. **e** Devo leggere questo libro? Non devo leggere questo libro.

Unit 3: a né **b** è **c** benché **d** sé **e** cioè **f** perché **g** poiché **h** tè **i** lo **j** d' **k** dall' **l** d' **m** un **n** un' **o** un' **p** un **q** un'

Unit 4: a un amico **b** un buon amico **c** quell'uomo **d** Qual è …? **e** buoni amici **f** poter andare **g** nessun amico **h** lavorar sodo **i** quel libro **j** to' **k** il signor Cervi **l** il dottor Green

Unit 5: a programma (m) **b** radio (f) **c** problema (m) **d** foto (f) **e** clima (m) **f** zia (f) **g** poeta (m) **h** tema (m) **i** moto(cicletta) (f)

Unit 6: a fiore **b** bambino **c** problema **d** uomo **e** mamma **f** gonna **g** banca **h** luce **i** strada **j** borsa **k** fungo **l** scatola

Unit 7: a lo **b** la **c** l' **d** lo **e** lo **f** lo **g** l' **h** lo **i** l' **j** lo **k** il

Unit 8: a la Cina **b** la Francia **c** l'Inghilterra **d** la signora Rossi **e** il signor Bianchi **f** Mi piacciono gli spaghetti.　**g** Abito in Toscana.　**h** Sean Connery è nato in Scozia?　**i** È Sean Connery!　**j** È la Loren!

Unit 9: a Costa 4 euro e 50 al litro.　**b** Costa venticinque sterline all'ora.　**c** È aumentato del dieci per cento. **d** Vado in montagna ogni anno.　**e** Mi piace vedere/guardare la televisione.　**f** Abito in campagna. **g** Vado in ufficio alle otto.

Unit 10: a un　**b** un　**c** un　**d** un　**e** uno　**f** uno **g** uno　**h** uno　**i** uno　**j** una　**k** una　**l** una　**m** un' **n** un'　**o** una　**p** una　**q** un'　**r** uno　**s** un'arancia **t** uno sci　**u** un uomo　**v** un'ape

Unit 11: a –　**b** –　**c** una　**d** un　**e** un　**f** –

Unit 12: a la fonte　**b** il fonte　**c** il boa　**d** la boa　**e** la pianta　**f** il pianto　**g** la foglia　**h** il tappo　**i** il mostro

Unit 13: a la ciclista, i ciclisti, le cicliste　**b** la turista, i turisti, le turiste　**c** la violinista, i violinisti, le violiniste **d** l'arpista, gli arpisti, le arpiste　**e** la pianista, i pianisti, le pianiste　**f** la collega, i colleghi, le colleghe　**g** l'atleta, gli atleti, le atlete　**h** la pediatra, i pediatri, le pediatre　**i** la psichiatra, gli psichiatri, le psichiatre　**j** la stratega, gli strateghi, le strateghe

Unit 14 (unchanged in the plural except for *moglie → mogli*): **a** le　**b** i　**c** le　**d** le　**e** le　**f** le　**g** le　**h** i　**i** le　**j** le **k** le　**l** le　**m** le　**n** i　**o** le　**p** i　**q** le mogli　**r** i　**s** gli **t** i　**u** i　**v** i　**w** gli　**x** i

Unit 15: ACROSS 3 muri 4 braccia 5 membra 6 ossi
DOWN 1 membri 2 bracci 5 mura 7 ossa

Unit 16: a 2 b 5 c 8 d 4 e 9 f 1 g 10 h 7
i 6 j 3

Unit 17: ACROSS 1 saliscendi 2 terrecotte 3 francobolli
4 cavalcavia DOWN 1 fabbriferrai 2 banconote
3 passaporti 4 benestare

Unit 18: a -e b -a c -a d -a e -i f -o
g -o/-o h -i

Unit 19: a Questa b Queste c Quest' d Questi
e Questa f Questi g Quella h Quelle i Quell'
j Quei k Quegli

Unit 20: a alcune riviste b alcune ore c alcuni giorni
d alcuni mesi e alcuni regali

Unit 21: a il b i c le d la e le f Il g Le h –

Unit 22: a Che b Quanti c Quante d Quanto
e Quale f Quali g Che
a 1 b 6 c 2 d 3 e 7 f 4 g 5

Unit 23: *See examples.*

Unit 24: a il/più b il più c le/meno d la più
e interessantissimo f velocissima g intelligentissima
h studiosissimo i noiosissimo j ostinatissima

Unit 25: a Quell' b Quella c Quell' d Quegli
e quel f quello g Quelle h Quel i gran
j grande k grandi l grande m grandi n gran

Unit 26: cinque, sei, sette, undici, dodici, tredici,
quattordici, quindici, sedici, diciassette, diciannove, venti,
ventisette, ventotto, trenta, trentasei, trentotto, cento-
quaranta, centosessantasette, millecinquecentosettantasei,
millesettecentosessantanove, duemilasei, sedicimilacinque-
centonovantasei, ventiseimilasettecento, centotrentasettemila-
settecentosessantasei, dieci milioni settecentocinquantotto-
milasettecentocinquantasei, cinque virgola otto, uno virgola
sei, tre virgola sette, quindici virgola nove, ventotto virgola
sei, settantaquattro virgola cinque, centoquindici virgola
nove, tremilaquattrocentocinquantasei virgola novantotto
a 2,27 b 2 c 4,39 d 1,55 e 2,78 f 3,41

Unit 27: a l'undicesimo capitolo b la nona sinfonia di
Beethoven c il terzo uomo d il diciassettesimo secolo
e la seconda strada a destra f la quarta figlia g il
secondo figlio h la terza tappa i la prima marcia j la
Quinta Strada k la terza (strada) a sinistra l il decimo
Comandamento

Unit 28: a true b true c true d true e false
f true g false

Unit 29: a mezzo b mezza c mezza d mezzo
e mezzo f mezz' g mezzo h mezza

Unit 30: a Ci vediamo lunedì.   b Ci vediamo la settimana prossima.   c Il martedì vado al cinema.   d Il mercoledì vado alla lezione d'italiano.   e Vado in discoteca la domenica.   f Il lunedì pomeriggio vado in palestra. g Il sabato mattina vado a cavalcare.   h Il venerdì sera vado a teatro.   i Che giorno è? È giovedì.   j Che data è oggi? È il primo giugno.

Unit 31: -are b cammino   d parlo   e guardo   g compro h ascolto   i volo   o ballo; -ere f vedo   j rido   k prendo l metto   m vivo   n piango; -ire a dormo   c parto

Unit 32: a Vedete?   b Non parlo tedesco.   c Parlano sempre di Lei.   d Parla sempre.   e Parli/Parla/Parlate/ Parlano inglese?   f Vedo mia madre ogni giorno/tutti i giorni.   g Vedi i miei occhiali?   h Abito qui da un anno. i Parti oggi?

Unit 33: a finiamo   b capiscono   c preferite d agiscono   e costruiscono   f puliscono

Unit 34: a Sono inglese.   b Io sono inglese, e Lei? c Esco, ti serve qualcosa?   d Io esco, e tu?

Unit 35: a Sì, la vedo.   b Sì, li vediamo.   c La domenica li vedo.   d Sì, vi vediamo.   e Lo prendo.   f Sì, la prendo.   g Sì, li prendo.   h Sì, mi aiuta.   i Li vediamo alla TV.   j Sì, ci aiutano.

Unit 36: a Eva ha fatto un regalo a me. Eva mi ha fatto un

regalo.   **b** Eva ha fatto un regalo a te. Eva ti ha fatto un regalo.
c Eva ha fatto un regalo a lui. Eva gli ha fatto un regalo.
d Eva ha fatto un regalo a lei. Eva le ha fatto un regalo.   **e** Eva
ha fatto un regalo a noi. Eva ci ha fatto un regalo.   **f** Eva ha
fatto un regalo a voi. Eva vi ha fatto un regalo.   **g** Eva ha fatto
un regalo a loro. Eva gli ha fatto un regalo/Eva ha fatto loro un
regalo.   **h** Le do un libro.   **i** Gli do un libro.   **j** Gli ho fatto/
Ho fatto loro una foto.   **k** Gli ho comprato/Ho comprato loro
un lampadario.   **l** Mi hanno comprato una valigia.   **m** Le ho
detto la verità.

Unit 37: a Te lo darò.   **b** Gliela darò.   **c** Glielo darò.
d Ve li darò.   **e** Gliela darò.   **f** Ve le darò.

Unit 38: a Mi ricordo di lui.   **b** Vado da lui.   **c** Chi
viene con lei?   **d** Marianna viene con noi.   **e** C'è una
lettera per voi.   **f** Non mi ricordo di lui.   **g** Non mi
ricordo di lei.   **h** Gisella viene con noi?   **i** C'è un
messaggio per te.   **j** Mi ricordo di lei.   **k** Questo pacco è
per te.   **l** Questi giornali sono per lui.

Unit 39: 1 è   **2** è   **3** È   **4** pagare   **5** sono   **6** sono
7 Ci sono   **8** ci sono   **9** c'è

Unit 40: Il signor Simoni scrive un libro. La signora Simoni
ha molti soldi e molti vestiti. Hanno un figlio e una figlia.
Marianna, la loro figlia, ha i capelli biondi e gli occhi
azzurri, e una barca. Ha ventitré anni. Ha molti amici.
Paolo, il loro figlio, ha vent'anni. Ha una veloce macchina

nuova. Hanno una grande casa con un giardino enorme.
Hanno anche una casa in campagna. Purtroppo hanno
sempre dei problemi.

Unit 41: a 4 b 6 c 7 d 8 e 2 f 1 g 3 h 5
i Chi va dal farmacista? j Da dove viene, signora? k Da
dove vieni, Robert? l Ti dispiace se vengo con te?
m Esco.

Unit 42: a beviamo b dicono c Diciamo d fa
e facciamo

Unit 43: a Quanti anni gli dai? b Che film danno alla
TV? c I Simoni danno una festa. d Sai giocare a tennis?
e Non sa giocare a carte. f Sanno che non posso andare.
g Mi dai il tuo video? h Non sappiamo la verità.

Unit 44: a 3 b 5 c 1 d 2 e 4

Unit 45: a possiamo b vuole c vogliono d vogliono
e possiamo f deve g dobbiamo h devo i devi

Unit 46: Transitive: *All except* dormire *and* piovere.
Active forms: a, d; **Passive forms:** b, c, c, f

Unit 47: a Marianna si trucca. b Ciccio non si alza
presto.

Unit 48: a Vuoi cambiarti la giacca? b Mi metto il
vestito. c Ti sei lavato le mani? d Il treno si è fermato a
Lucca. e La finestra si è aperta. f Giulia ha aperto la

finestra. **g** Quell'uomo è pieno di sé. **h** L'auto si è fermata e la portiera si è aperta. **i** L'allarme ha fermato il treno. **j** Giulia non crede in se stessa.
k È andata lei stessa.

Unit 49: a Il negozio è chiuso. **b** La farmacia è aperta.
c Ho visto il film due volte. **d** Ho scritto una lettera.
e Ho preso una casa in Toscana. **f** Ho fatto una torta.
g Ha vissuto bene. **h** Ho permesso a Marina di uscire.
i Ho letto il libro. **j** Ho camminato per tre chilometri.

Unit 50: a Sono andata **b** sono andati **c** siamo andati
d abbiamo impiegato **e** Siamo arrivati **f** abbiamo fatto
g ci siamo seduti **h** abbiamo preso

Unit 51: a è **b** è **c** ha **d** è **e** hanno
f siamo/siete/sono **g** abbiamo **h** Ho dovuto camminare per due miglia. **i** Sono dovuti partire/andare via presto.
j Hai parlato al dottore? **k** Sei uscito(-a)/Siete usciti(-e) ieri sera? **l** Abbiamo guardato la partita di calcio alla TV.
m L'ho visto ieri. **n** Glielo hanno detto subito. **o** Gli ha telefonato da Napoli. **p** Hanno parlato al presidente.
q Abbiamo vissuto in India per tre anni.

Unit 52: a ero; volevo **b** Suonavo; ero **c** andavo
d Nuotavo **e** Mangiavo **f** studiavo; ascoltavo;
mangiavo **g** uscivo **h** parlavamo **i** ritornavo

Unit 53: a ci vuole **b** ci vogliono **c** ci vuole **d** ci vuole **e** ci vogliono **f** ci vuole

Unit 54: a piace **b** piace **c** piace **d** piacciono
e piacciono **f** piace **g** piacciono; piacciono **h** piace

Unit 55: a Leggerò il libro domani. **b** Il treno partirà tra
poco. **c** L'autobus arriverà tra poco. **d** Studierò la
lezione domani. **e** Andrò a piedi domani. **f** Domani
rimarrò a casa. **g** Le telefonerò domani. **h** La vedrò
domani.

Unit 56: a Studierei ma sono stanca. **b** Scriveremmo ma
non abbiamo tempo. **c** Finiremmo ma è troppo tardi.
d Partirebbero ma non hanno i soldi. **e** Guarderebbero la
TV ma hanno altro da fare. **f** Verrebbe ma non ha tempo.

Unit 57: a 4 **b** 6 **c** 3 **d** 5 **e** 2· **f** 1

Unit 58: a Scrivigli la lettera. **b** Raccontagli tutto.
c Le venda la macchina. **d** Gli compri un nuovo
computer. **e** Gli consigli di stare a casa. **f** Parlategli del
fatto. **g** Mandategli i documenti.

Unit 59: 1 a Dalle il libro! **b** Vai/Va' via! **c** Di' la
verità! **d** Fa' attenzione! **e** Fa' presto! **2 a** Le dia il
libro! **b** Vada via! **c** Dica la verità! **d** Faccia
attenzione! **e** Faccia presto! **3 a** 3 **b** 2 **c** 1 **d** 4

Unit 60: a venda **b** abbia **c** partano **d** meriti
e vendano **f** piova

Unit 61: a vendesse **b** avesse **c** partissero **d** meritasse
e vendessero **f** piovesse **g** mangiassi **h** avesse

Unit 62: a Insistevano che noi andassimo via/partissimo subito. **b** Ho paura che il bambino abbia preso il raffreddore. **c** Avevo paura che il bambino avesse preso il raffreddore. **d** Ci tiene molto che lui finisca il lavoro.

Unit 63: Present: a, c, f, h; **Imperfect:** b, d, e, g, i, **j** stessero **k** togliessi **l** esca **m** uscisse

Unit 64: a Garibaldi nacque a Nizza nel 1807. **b** Dopo che ebbe partecipato ad un attentato per conquistare Genova, dovette fuggire in Sud America. **c** Quando ritornò partecipò alla lotta per l'Unità d'Italia.

Unit 65: *Past definite:* alzò, avvicinò, pensò, osservò, cominciò, accorse, suonò, alzò, salì *Imperfect:* riusciva, faceva *Pluperfect:* erano appassiti, avevano accumulato, avevano cambiato *Perfect:* ha scritto

Unit 66: a parlando **b** Sbagliando **c** lavorando **d** Continuando **e** Avendo

Unit 67: a Paolo è sempre sorridente. **b** Francesco è un uomo abbiente. **c** Questo treno è proveniente da Roma? **d** Era un film divertente. **e** Conosci l'amante di Maria? **f** Giovanni è uno studente brillante. **g** il sole nascente **h** la luna calante

Unit 68: a vivere **b** parlare **c** spendere **d** fumare **e** venire **f** continuare **g** pensare

Unit 69: a compongo, componi, compone, componiamo, componete, compongono **b** attrassi, attraesti, attrasse, attraemmo, attraeste, attrassero **c** traduci!, traduca!, traduciamo!, traducete!, traducano! **d** traduco, traduci, traduce, traduciamo, traducete, traducono

Unit 70: a Se lo fa. **b** Se la fa. **c** Se la prepara. **d** Se li stira.

Unit 71: a 8 **b** 7 **c** 6 **d** 5 **e** 4 **f** 3 **g** 2 **h** 1

Unit 72: a Teresa impara/sta imparando a suonare il piano. **b** Paolo ci tiene molto a giocare a tennis. **c** Non vedo l'ora di vederti. **d** Siamo stufi di tradurre questi esercizi. **e** Erano sicuri di aver ragione.

Unit 73: a Con questo rumore è difficile lavorare. **b** Prendo il caffè con due cucchiaini di zucchero. **c** Paolo è arrivato con l'automobile di sua madre. **d** Marianna è stata gentile con loro. **e** Eleonora ha deciso di andare al cinema con la sua amica. **f** Con mia grande sorpresa ha accettato l'invito. **g** Dovrebbero imparare a prenderla con calma. **h** Ieri sono andata al cinema con lui.

Unit 74: a della **b** del **c** della **d** dei; degli; delle **e** della **f** dello **g** del **h** della

Unit 75: a a scuola **b** all'aeroporto **c** alla spiaggia

Unit 76: a 4 **b** 7 **c** 3 **d** 2 **e** 1 **f** 5 **g** 6

Unit 77: a Il telefono è sul tavolo. **b** La penna è sulla rivista. **c** Sul televisore c'è un gatto. **d** Sulla rivista c'è scritto *Gente*. **e** Ho visto le notizie/il telegiornale alla televisione.

Unit 78: a 6 **b** 3 **c** 4 **d** 2 **e** 5 **f** 7 **g** 1 **h** 9 **i** 8

Unit 79: a 4 **b** 5 **c** 3 **d** 1 **e** 9 **f** 6 **g** 7 **h** 2 **i** 8 **j** 10

Unit 80: a una macchina da cucire **b** una lampada da tavolo **c** una macchina da scrivere **d** una lampadina da sessanta watts **e** un gelato da due euro

Unit 81: a davanti alla casa **b** in cima alla collina **c** dietro la casa **d** vicino alla macchina **e** La macchina/L'auto si è fermata in mezzo alla strada. **f** Erano tutti presenti ad eccezione di due. **g** Non potevo sentire a causa del rumore. **h** Lucca è lontano da qui? **i** La fontana è vicino alla Basilica. **j** Oggi la sterlina è in rialzo rispetto al dollaro.

Unit 82: a chiaramente **b** male **c** velocemente **d** difficilmente **e** grandemente **f** rapidamente **g** magnificamente **h** inutilmente **i** probabilmente **j** agilmente **k** gentilmente **l** maggiormente **m** fortemente **n** duramente **o** elegantemente **p** ovviamente **q** cortesemente **r** mollemente

Unit 83: a 6 **b** 4 **c** 5 **d** 2 **e** 3 **f** 1 **g** 7

Unit 84: 1 a È una persona che si emoziona facilmente.
b D'estate piove raramente. c Parla italiano
correntemente. d Se vuoi farti capire devi parlare
lentamente e chiaramente. e Ha continuato a negare
fermamente. f Vedo che hai studiato diligentemente.
g Non ho ancora finito. 2 a Ha sempre lavorato
onestamente. b Rispose debolmente alla mia domanda.
c Ho già letto quel libro. d Non è molto ricco
interiormente. 3 a probabilmente b possibilmente
c lontano

Unit 86: a 8 b 9 c 7 d 6 e 5 f 4 g 3 h 2
i 1

Unit 87: a Che coraggio! b Che stupido! c Meno
male! d Accidenti che sfortuna! e Che bugiardo che sei!
f Dai, vallo a raccontare ad un altro!

Unit 88: a Non c'era molta gente. b Non c'è mai molta
gente. c Non ha niente da fare. d Non ha mai niente da
fare. e Non sa niente. f Non sa mai niente. g Non mi
piace per niente. h Non mi ha ringraziato. i No, non mi
sono piaciuti. j No, non ci è piaciuto. k No, non lo
vedo mai. l No, non c'era nessumo. m No, non ho
niente. n No, non gioco più.

Unit 89: a finché non b a meno che non c finché non
d finché non e a meno che non f Questa medicina è
controindicata per i sofferenti di cuore. g Quel

macchinario è in disuso dall'anno scorso. **h** Spero di riuscire. **i** Il governo ha deciso di decentralizzare i servizi pubblici.

Unit 90: **a** 5 **b** 4 **c** 8 **d** 3 **e** 6 **f** 2 **g** 1 **h** 7 **i** da cui **j** in cui **k** per cui **l** con/in cui **m** a cui

Unit 91: **a** Abbiamo comprato tutto ciò/tutto quello che abbiamo potuto. **b** Ciò/Quello che fa non mi riguarda. **c** Ciò/Quello che conta è la salute. **b** Ciò/Quello che dicono è falso. **e** Le hanno dato tutto quello che/tutto ciò che avevano. **f** Questo è tutto quello che/tutto ciò che puoi fare? **g** Questo è tutto quello che/tutto ciò che so. **h** Hanno preso tutto ciò che/tutto quello che c'era.

Unit 92: **a** nessuno **b** niente **c** Ciascuno **d** qualcosa **e** qualcuno **f** qualcun **g** uno **h** Chiunque

Unit 93: **1 a** Chi **b** Chi **c** Quali **d** Che cosa **e** Che cosa **f** Che cosa **g** Qual **h** Che cosa **i** Che **j** Chi **k** Quale/Che cosa/Chi **2 a** 4 **b** 5 **c** 6 **d** 3 **e** 7 **f** 2 **g** 1 **3 a** Qual è tuo marito? **b** Che lavoro fai? **c** Chi è andato alla festa? **d** Che cosa hai visto? **e** Qual è il tuo cappotto? **f** Che cosa vogliono?

Unit 94: **a** 8 **b** 1 **c** 6 **d** 7 **e** 5 **f** 3 **g** 2 **h** 4

Unit 95: **a** 4 **b** 3 **c** 8 **d** 5 **e** 6 **f** 7 **g** 1 **h** 2 **i** 9 **j** A chi tocca? **k** Che cosa danno al cinema?

l Che cos'hai?/Come ti senti? m Che tipi ha?/Quanti tipi ne ha? n Che cos'ha/hai? o E perché? p Da dove viene/vieni? q Dov'è il gatto? r A che ora comincia la partita? s Di chi è l'ombrello?

Unit 96: a 4 b 5 c 6 d 1 e 2 f 3 g 10
h 9 i 7 j 8

Exercise 1 (Unit 1)

Using the words in the box complete the sentences to give a title to each of the four pictures.

a La mamma _____   **c** Il treno _____
b I libri che ho ordinato _____ **d** Mariella _____

Il treno delle 6.45	arriverà	una lettera
The 6.45 train	*(it) will arrive*	*a letter*

La mamma
Mum   la settimana prossima   arriveranno
next week   *(they) will arrive*   presto
soon

scrive
is writing   il pasto   Mariella
the meal   *Mariella*

prepara   per il bambino
is preparing   I libri che ho ordinato   *for the child*
the books I ordered

Exercise 2 (Unit 2)

Form four sentences taking the words from the box below, using this example as a pattern.

E.g. Angelo vive in una casa grande.

adjectives	nouns	verbs
interessante *interesting*	Francesco/un cantante *singer*	ha *has*
blu *blue*	Elisa/un libro *book*	legge *is reading*
enorme *enormous*	Filippo/un'automobile *car*	è *is*
famoso *famous*	Mario/un vestito *suit*	indossa *wears*

Exercise 3 (Unit 4)

Correct the expressions below by dropping the final vowel or syllable when possible.

a il male di denti
b la prova scritta
c il male di testa
d il male di cuore
e il Mare Adriatico
f un cuore d'oro
g quale è?
h stai attento
i un poco di vino

Quel bel ragazzo ha un cuor d'oro!

Exercise 4 (Unit 5)

Write the name and gender (m. or f.) under each picture.

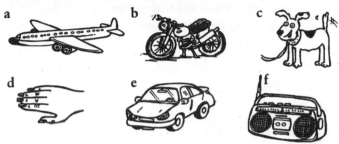

a

b

c

d

e

f

Exercise 5 (Unit 6)

Below is a list of nouns: some take an -h between the -c or -g and the plural ending, others do not. Can you sort them out?

farmaco	buco	porco	banca	amico
	greco	stomaco	medico	

Exercise 6 (Unit 6)

Give the plural of the following nouns. The stressed vowel is <u>underlined</u>.

a viaggio (*trip/voyage*)
b figlio (*son/child*)
c zio (*uncle*)
d leggio (*book rest/music stand*)
e specchio (*mirror*)
f brusio (*buzz/hum*)

Exercise 7 (Unit 8)

Make questions by joining each verb in the box to each of the adjectives of nationality listed below.

E.g. Parla tedesco? Studia il tedesco?

Parla	Studia

a francese	*French*	f portoghese	*Portuguese*	k polacco	*Polish*
b inglese	*English*	g turco	*Turkish*	l danese	*Danish*
c tedesco	*German*	h arabo	*Arabic*	m svedese	*Swedish*
d spagnolo	*Spanish*	i russo	*Russian*	n norvegese	*Norwegian*
e greco	*Greek*	j olandese	*Dutch*	o finlandese	*Finnish*

Exercise 8 (Unit 9)

Translate the following expressions into Italian and then read them aloud (see vocabulary below).

a Soave wine costs 4 euros 50 per litre.
b I like watching football on television.
c Ninety per cent of the population has a car.
d A lesson costs £25 per hour.
e Imperial Rome
f Dinner is ready.
g What time is breakfast?

il calcio	*football*	**pronto**	*ready*
la cena	*dinner*	**la colazione**	*breakfast*

Exercise 9 (Unit 11)

Translate the following into Italian.

a What a pity!
b half a kilo (**chilo**) of apples (**mele**)
c half an hour
d a hundred times
e six hours a day
f twice a day
g half a pint (**pinta**)
h what a handsome lad!

Translate the following into Italian.

i I have (**Ho**) a sore throat.
j I have a headache.
k Andrea has (**ha**) toothache.
l Goffredo has (**ha**) a cold.
m Angela has a terrible cold.
n I am in (**Ho**) such a hurry!
o I have such an appetite!
p As a child I was a tomboy.

Exercise 10 (Unit 12)

Complete each phrase with the correct word preceded by the definite or indefinite article as suggested by the English translation.

a _____ di Trionfo (*the Arc de Triomphe*)
b Ho _____ portatile. (*I have a portable radio.*)
c _____ d'interesse è sceso. (*The rate of interest has gone down.*)
d _____ della pentola (*the handle of the saucepan*)
e _____ di carta (*a sheet of paper*)
f _____ è arrivata? (*Has the mail arrived?*)
g Questa bottiglia è senza _____. (*This bottle is without a cork.*)
h Londra è _____ dell'Inghilterra. (*London is the capital of England.*)
i _____ del Tour de France (*the stages of the Tour de France*)
j _____ di fico (*a fig leaf*)

Exercise 11 (Unit 13)

Sort these nouns into three groups: masculine, feminine and common gender.

a violinista   b cavalla   c casa   d collega   e gatto   f borsista
g problema   h bufalo   i cerva   j infanticida   k radio
l ritrattista   m maschio della giraffa   n gatta
o femmina del leopardo   p libro   q arco   r posto   s cantante
t posta   u mostra   v zoo

Exercise 12 (Unit 14)

Write the opposite gender/article for the nouns below.

E.g. Il padre → la madre

a l'uomo   c la moglie   e la nuora
b la sorella   d il celibe/lo scapolo   f il maschio

Write the plural form of the following nouns and articles.

E.g. la bontà → le bontà

g la qualità   i la virtù   k il caffè
h la quantità   j la città   l il tè

Exercise 13 (Unit 15)

Translate the following expressions into Italian.

a one mile   b two miles   c about one hundred persons
(_____ **di persone**)   d ten fingers (**dieci** _____)   e about
one thousand dollars (_____ **di dollari**)   f some thousands

of miles (**alcune** _____ **di** _____) **g** one finger

Exercise 14 (Unit 16)

What would you call these?

Exercise 15 (Unit 17)

Complete the words to give the meanings as shown.

a capo _____ (*masterpieces*) **b** capo _ _____ (*paragraphs*)
c capo _____ (*dizzy spells*) **d** capi _____ (*group leaders*)
e capi _____ (*foremen*) **f** capi _____ (*chief technicians*)
g capi _____ (*station masters*) **h** capi _____ (*leaders of a file (of people)*)

Exercise 16 (Unit 18)

Pair the nouns on the following page to their related adjectives.

E.g. commercio → commerciale

a l'economia	l lo spazio	1 spazioso	12 americano
b l'industria	m il presidente	2 statunitense	13 economico
c Milano	n il peso	3 studioso	14 paziente
d l'America	o il gusto	4 presidenziale	15 climatico
e gli Stati Uniti	p l'aroma	5 operoso	16 milanese
f l'Italia	q la pazienza	6 sportivo	17 inglese
g l'Inghilterra	r il clima	7 generoso	18 intelligente
h lo studio	s la generosità	8 bello	19 industriale
i la bellezza	t l'opera	9 italiano	20 pesante
j l'intelligenza	u l'acqua	10 annuale	21 gustoso
k l'anno	v lo sport	11 acquatico	22 aromatico

Exercise 17 (Unit 19)

Say the following aloud in Italian.

a I want (**Voglio**) this one (*m.*).   b I take (**Prendo**) these (*m.*).
c I don't want (**Non voglio**) that one (*m.*).   d I am not taking
(**Non prendo**) those (*f.*).

Exercise 18 (Unit 20)

**How often do you do these things? Choose the right
expression from the box to complete each sentence.**

> ogni giorno (*day*)   ogni settimana (*week*)   ogni mese (*month*)
> ogni tre mesi (*three months*)   ogni anno (*year*)

Devo pagare (*I must pay*) …
a … il lattaio (*the milkman*) _____ .
b … la bolletta del telefono (*phone bill*) _____ .
c … la tassa di circolazione (*road tax*) _____ .
d … la segretaria (*the secretary*) _____ .

Exercise 19 (Unit 21)

Change the English adjectives or pronouns into their corresponding Italian forms.

a Quelli sono (*our*) libri.

b Questa è (*their*) casa.

c (*My*) ufficio è in via Garibaldi.

d Quei quadri sono (*his*), non (*mine*).

e (*my*) sorella maggiore

f (*her*) fratellino

g (*Your* (informal)) babbo è qui.

h (*Your* (formal)) quadri sono falsi.

Exercise 20 (Unit 23)

Match these expressions with their English translation.

a il più possibile

b il meno possibile

c il più presto possibile

d sempre più

e sempre meno

f più o meno

1 as much as possible

2 less and less

3 more and more

4 as little as possible

5 more or less

6 as soon as possible

Exercise 21 (Unit 27)

Now read aloud the titles of the following popes and monarchs.

a Papa Paolo VI

b Pio IX

c Leone X

d Giovanni XXIII

e Giovanni Paolo II

f Re Vittorio Emanuele III

g Gustavo XVI

h Giorgio VI

i Enrico IV

j Regina Elisabetta II

Exercise 22 (Unit 28)

Translate the following into Italian.

a According to some (*Secondo alcuni*), the third millennium goes from the 1st January 2000 to the 31st December 2999.
b Dante is the great poet of the 1200s.
c The present (**attuale**) century is called (**si chiama**) the 21st century.

Exercise 23 (Unit 29)

Write these fractions in full and then read them aloud.

a $\frac{1}{2}$
b $\frac{2}{3}$
c $\frac{3}{4}$
d $\frac{5}{8}$
e $\frac{7}{8}$
f $\frac{4}{5}$
g $\frac{5}{16}$
h $\frac{19}{32}$
i $\frac{5}{6}$
j $\frac{9}{10}$

Read aloud the following sums.

E.g. 5 + 5 = 10 → **Cinque più cinque fa dieci.**
5 – 5 = 0 → **Cinque meno cinque fa zero.**
5 × 5 = 25 → **Cinque per cinque fa venticinque.**
5 : 5 = 1 → **Cinque diviso cinque fa uno.**

k 5 + 12 = 17
l 10 – 6 = 4
m 10 × 10 = 100
n 12 : 2 = 6
o 45 – 30 = 15
p 125 × 75 = 9.375
q 136 : 5 = 27,2
r 451 : 8 = 56,37

Exercise 24 (Unit 30)

Fill in the gaps with your own responses.
a Oggi è _____.   b Sono nato(-a) il _____.   c Il mese che preferisco è _____.   d La stagione che preferisco è _____.
e Di solito vado in vacanza _____.

Exercise 25 (Unit 33)

Write down the correct form of the verb e.g. (io) salire → salgo
a (lui) salire   b (noi) salire   c (loro) tenere   d (loro) spegnere   e (io) spegnere   f (tu) tenere   g (loro) tenere
h (noi) tenere   i (voi) scegliere   j (io) rimanere   k (loro) scegliere   l (tu) rimanere

Exercise 26 (Unit 34)

How would you translate these sentences? Remember you need to use the present tense.

E.g. Are *you* going to buy the bananas? → Comprate *voi* le banane?

a I am answering!

| *to answer* **rispondere** |

b Are you (*fam. sing.*) answering?
c Is he going to answer?
d Are you (*fam. sing.*) going to buy the cards (**cartoline**)?
e Are you (*fam. pl.*) going to buy the cards?
f Yes, we will buy the cards.

Exercise 27 (Unit 35)

Enter the last vowel of the verb.

E.g. Hai preso il treno? L'ho pres_____ . → L'ho preso.

a Hai preso l'autobus?   L'ho pres_____ .
b Avete preso le mele?   Le abbiamo pres_____ .
c Hanno comprato l'automobile? L'hanno comprat_____ .
d Gianni ha venduto la casa?   L'ha vendut_____ .

Exercise 28 (Unit 37)

Write the alternative forms of the direct and indirect pronouns followed by *dovere*, *potere*, *volere* + infinitive.

a Lo voglio vedere.   f Lo devo leggere.
b Gli voglio parlare.   g Lo posso vedere?
c Le voglio telefonare.   h Gli posso telefonare?
d Vi devo scrivere.   i Ci puoi scrivere?
e Ci deve vedere.

Exercise 29 (Unit 38)

Translate into Italian using *ci*.

a Is there a supermarket (**supermercato**) near here?
b I go there every month.
c I come here once a year.
d We always think about them.
e There are seven days in one week.

Exercise 30 (Unit 39)
Answer the following questions.

E.g. La signora è in treno? → Sì, è in treno.

a Maria è in discoteca?   c Il signor Simoni è in banca?
b Sono in classe i ragazzi?   d Marianna e Paolo sono italiani?

Now answer the questions in the negative.

E.g. New York è in Europa? → No, non è in Europa.

e Io sono alla partita?   g Marianna e Paolo sono a casa?
f Siamo a Capri?   h Sei alla mensa?

Exercise 31 (Unit 40)

Match the questions and answers or the two halves of the sentences.

a Ha i documenti?   1 No, non li ho.
b Hai fame?   2 … una casa in campagna.
c Tu hai torto …   3 Sì, un po'; hai un
                         panino (*a roll*)?
d Avete dei problemi?   4 … e io ho ragione.
e Paolo e Marianna hanno sete.   5 Hai dell'acqua minerale?
f C'è un albergo in questa strada? 6 Ne abbiamo molti.
g I signori Simoni hanno …   7 Sì, a duecento metri,
                                      a destra.

Exercise 32 (Unit 42)

Fill the spaces under the pictures.

a _____ molto _____ . b Roberta _____ le valigie. c Loro _____ i biglietti.

Exercise 33 (Unit 43)

Fill the blanks with the correct person of the verbs *dare* and *sapere*.

a Che cosa _____ al cinema oggi?
b (Tu) mi _____ la macchina?
c I ragazzi _____ una festa sabato prossimo.
d Quanti anni gli _____ ?
e Tu _____ tutto, io non _____ nulla.
f (Lei) _____ quattro lingue.
g (Io) _____ che si è sposato.

Exercise 34 (Unit 44)

Using the information in Unit 44, give the other half of the questions/answers opposite.

a _____ ?   Bene grazie, e Lei?
b _____ ?   Sto all'albergo Regina.
c Com'è il tuo bambino?   È molto bello ma _____ .
d _____ ?   Oggi non sto molto bene.

Exercise 35 (Unit 45)

Match each question with an appropriate answer.

a Vuole parlare al mio collega?   1 Lo devo ai miei genitori.
b Volete aprire la porta?   2 No, potete venire domani.
c Puoi venire da me (*to me*) domani? 3 Sì, è urgente.
d Può chiudere il finestrino?   4 Certamente, signora.
e Potete stare zitti, per favore?   5 No, voglio parlare al direttore.
f Dobbiamo venire subito?   6 Certo, ci scusi.
g Devo farlo oggi?   7 Ci dispiace (*We're sorry*),
h A chi deve il suo successo?   non possiamo aprirla.
                                     8 Posso ma non voglio.

Exercise 36 (Unit 49)

**Write the irregular past participles of the infinitives below,
then read them aloud e.g. leggere → letto.**

a venire b rompere c offrire d correre e fare
f mettere g bere h prendere i vedere j rimanere
k aprire l essere m chiudere n scrivere o nascere
p muovere q leggere r dire s scendere t vivere.

Exercise 37 (Unit 50)

Translate the following into Italian.

a I have been on holiday
   with Claire.
b We took the boat to San Fruttuoso.
c We have been walking all day.
d We did some shopping.
e We went to a disco.

f We drank a coffee and
   went out.
g They caught the train.
h They returned home last week.
i She arrived at Portofino.
j The thief (**ladro**) escaped.

Exercise 38 (Unit 52)

Read the passage then change the present tense into the imperfect.

I miei nonni (**a** abitano) in una casa in collina. D'estate, quando (**b** iniziano) le vacanze, (**c** vado) a vivere con loro per una settimana o due. La casa (**d** è) a soli venti minuti di distanza dal centro della cittadina ma lassù (*up there*) (**e** c'è) un'atmosfera molto diversa: in centro (**f** si può) uscire e subito (**g** ci sono) i negozi e molte persone a cui parlare o da salutare (*to greet*). (**h** Basta) scendere una scala per trovarsi immediatamente al mare che, dalla finestra di casa, (**i** si vede) proprio vicino. La casa dei nonni (**j** è) isolata, circondata (*surrounded*) da grandi muri come le poche ville nel vicinato. (**k** C'è) soltanto un negozio che (**l** vende) un po' di tutto. (**m** Si vede) pochissima gente nella stradina che (**n** conduce) (*leads*) in quella zona: le macchine non (**o** possono) entrare. (**p** C'è) molto silenzio specialmente dopo il pranzo quando i nonni (**q** vanno) a riposare. (**r** Si sentono) soltanto le cicale (*cicadas*). Io (**s** gioco) con il gattino oppure (*or*) (**t** osservo) le lucertole (*lizards*) che, sui muri di cinta, (**u** si scaldano) (*warm up*) al sole.

Exercise 39 (Unit 53)

With the help of the words in brackets, answer these questions, choosing between *basta* or *bastano*.

E.g. Quanto sale (*salt*)? (un grammo) → Ne (*of it*) basta un grammo.

Quante carote? (due) → Ne (*of them*) bastano due.

È difficile superare l'esame? → No, basta studiare.

a Quanto zucchero? (due cucchiaini)
b Quanto vino? (mezzo bicchiere)
c Quanti funghi? (cento grammi)
d È difficile imparare? (studiare)
e È difficile da trovare? (avere la carta stradale)

Exercise 40 (Unit 54)

What do Cristina and Marco like or dislike?

E.g. A Cristina non piace il calcio, a Marco piace la televisione.

Exercise 41 (Unit 55)

Below is a list of things you want to do when you are in the Seychelles. Change the verb from the present to the future tense.

Quando andrò alle Seychelles …
a nuoto almeno due ore al giorno.
b mi abbronzo moltissimo.
c leggo molti libri sulla spiaggia.
d faccio nuove conoscenze.
e prendo a nolo una barca.
f scrivo ai miei amici.
g non guardo le notizie alla TV.
h non leggo i giornali.

Exercise 42 (Unit 56)

Translate the following into Italian.
a I'd like a beer and a roll.
b I'd love to go on holiday.
c You (*inform. sing.*) ought to tell him.
d I couldn't do it.
e He wouldn't do it.

Exercise 43 (Unit 58)

Using the sentences you wrote for the exercises in Unit 58, change the direct object pronoun to the appropriate pronoun *lo, la, li, le, ci* or *ne*.

E.g. Mandaglielo. Telefonagliela.

Now write the negative form of the above sentences.

E.g. Non mandare il pacco a Marianna.
Non telefonare la notizia a Paolo.

Exercise 44 (Unit 60)

Change the underlined verb into the correct form of the perfect subjunctive.

E.g. Credo che lui <u>partire</u> ieri. → Credo che <u>sia partito</u> ieri.

a Spero che loro **comprare** un'auto nuova.
b Lo aiutano sebbene non lo **meritare**.
c Nonostante io **mangiare** moltissimo non sono ingrassata.
d Credo che la festa **avere** luogo ieri.
e Immagino che lei **vendere** le azioni (*shares*).

Exercise 45 (Unit 61)

Match the two halves of the sentences.

a Se fossi in te ...   1 se li avessi.
b Se Marcello avesse mangiato di più ...2 fossi partito in treno.
c Non avrei mai immaginato ...   3 che fossero così scorretti.
d Avrei voluto ...   4 fosse il suo compleanno.
e Credevo che domani ...   5 adesso sarebbe più grasso.
f Pensavo che il professore ...   6 cambierei casa.
g Supponevo che tu ...   7 che loro venissero.
h Ti darei volentieri i libri ...   8 mi avrebbe aiutato a scrivere
                                                              una lettera all'Ambasciatore.

Exercise 46 (Unit 62)

Match the two halves of the sentences.

a È giusto che ...   1 ... finisca i compiti prima di uscire.
b Mi fa piacere che voi ...   2 ... prima che sia troppo tardi.
c Cogli (*take*) l'opportunità ... 3 ... tu chieda scusa.
d È meglio che Mario ...   4 ... superino (*pass*) l'esame.
e È ingiusto ...   5 ... abbiate accettato l'invito.
f È necessario che ...   6 ... che gli studenti siano
                                                          promossi se non hanno studiato.

Exercise 47 (Unit 63)

Translate the following into Italian.
a I want you to go out more.
b I think they want to move (**cambiare casa**).
c I thought he would come.
d I think he keeps it in the desk.
e If they had to choose, they would go to France.

Exercise 48 (Unit 64)

Add the missing verbs to the passage below.
Garibaldi, patriota italiano, **a** _____ a Nizza nel 1807. Si unì
al movimento 'Giovane Italia' e **b** _____ condannato a morte
per aver partecipato ad un attentato per conquistare Genova.
Fuggì in Sud America e **c** _____ in Italia nel 1849 ma dovette
fuggire un'altra volta. Dopo avere lavorato a New York, **d**
_____ in Italia nel 1854. Nel 1859 tornò a combattere per la
libertà d'Italia e nel 1860 si **e** _____ all'isola di Caprera dove
f _____ fino alla morte.

Exercise 49 (Unit 66)

Replace *dopo*, *mentre*, *siccome* + verb with the gerund.
E.g. Siccome sono arrivata in anticipo (*early*) non ho trovato
nessuno. → Essendo arrivata in anticipo non ho trovato nessuno.
a Siccome non era stanco è andato a piedi.
b Siccome i negozi erano chiusi è andato al ristorante.
c Dopo aver comprato i biglietti sono tornato a casa.

d Dopo avere commesso tale gaffe preferì tacere per il resto della serata.

e Mentre attraversava la strada inciampò e cadde (*he stumbled and fell*).

f Mentre usciva di casa decise di prendere l'ombrello.

Exercise 50 (Unit 67)

Translate the following using the present participles/nouns from Unit 67.

a Francesco is an important manager.

b During (**Durante**) the last century, many Italian emigrants went to America.

c Both contestants are very good.

d He is an acquaintance of mine.

e My washing machine is not working (**non funziona**).

f I want a new fishing rod for Christmas.

Exercise 51 (Unit 68)

Translate the following into Italian.

a They go swimming every day.

b Marianne and Paul go fishing when they can.

c I'm tired of repeating the same things.

d They did not succeed in convincing him (**convincerlo**).

Exercise 52 (Unit 69)

Change the verbs in brackets into the corresponding Italian one.

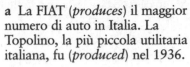

a La FIAT (*produces*) il maggior numero di auto in Italia. La Topolino, la più piccola utilitaria italiana, fu (*produced*) nel 1936.

b Ho (*placed*) le scatole l'una sull'altra. Se ci fosse stato più spazio le avrei (*placed*) una accanto all'altra

c Goffredo (*draws*) ispirazione dalla natura per i suoi quadri. I suoi studenti (*draw*) esempio dalle sue opere. Lui ha (*exhibited*) le sue opere alla Galleria d'Arte Moderna. I suoi allievi di solito (*exhibit*) nell'Aula Magna dell'università.

Exercise 53 (Unit 70)

Match the two halves of the sentences.

a Devo andarmene perché …
b Si è mangiato …
c Se li è mangiati …
d Si dice che lei sia …
e Non si è mai troppo …

1 … una donna molto potente.
2 … vecchi per imparare.
3 … appartamenti.
4 … l'un l'altro.
5 … tedesco e spagnolo.

f	Si affittano (*to let*) …	6	… tutti.
g	I nostri studenti si rispettano …	7	… si è fatto tardi.
h	Qui si parla inglese, francese, …	8	… due porzioni di ravioli.

Exercise 54 (Unit 71)

Below is a list of activities, sports and pastimes that you may like or dislike. Make a sentence for each one of them.

E.g. Mi piace nuotare. Non mi piace giocare a rugby.

giocare a tennis   andare in bicicletta   leggere   visitare i musei   visitare le gallerie d'arte   viaggiare   giocare a carte giocare a pallacanestro (*basketball*)   studiare l'italiano andare a pesca   andare in discoteca   ascoltare la musica dipingere   giocare a scacchi (*chess*)   dormire   ballare cavalcare (*horse riding*)   scrivere

Exercise 55 (Unit 72)

Add the preposition *a* or *di* as appropriate.

Renzo pensava **a** _____ prendersi una vacanza. Sua moglie lo aveva incoraggiato **b** _____ raggiungerlo al mare ma lui si era impegnato **c** _____ fare degli affari (*business*) molto importanti per la sua ditta e tardava **d** _____ prendere una decisione. D'altra parte (*On the other hand*) non voleva rinunciare **e** _____ riposarsi un po' dopo un lungo inverno di lavoro senza pausa. 'Se ti ostini **f** _____ lavorare così, ti ammalerai, gli diceva sua moglie nel tentativo (*attempting*) di persuaderlo **g** _____ desistere. Però lui ci teneva talmente (*so much*) **h** _____ suo lavoro che seguitava ad andare in ufficio

anche il sabato. Certo sua moglie aveva ragione i _____
insistere e anche il dottore che gli aveva consigliato
j _____ lavorare di meno, però lui sognava di comprare una
bella casa per la sua famiglia e tentava k _____ rimandare il
riposo ed i divertimenti al futuro. Fermò la macchina e scese
per comprare un rivista. 'D'altra parte', pensava, seguitando
l _____ ragionare su questo argomento 'se andassi al mare,
sarei obbligato m _____ passare molto tempo sulla spiaggia,
sotto l'ombrellone, mentre io preferirei di gran lunga (*by far*)
essere in montagna'. Si rendeva conto n _____ essere
esagerato nella sua ostinazione o _____ trovare scuse e non
vedeva l'ora p _____ trovare una soluzione o perlomeno un
compromesso. E la soluzione la trovò quando …

Exercise 56 (Unit 73)

Add either *a(d)*, *di* or *con*, to the sentences below.

a Devi affrettarti _____ andare.
b Crede sempre _____ avere ragione.
c Sono stata in Corsica _____ la nave traghetto (*ferry boat*).
d Faresti meglio _____ studiare di più.
e Vieni al cinema _____ me?
f Ho il passaporto _____ me.
g Prendo un bicchiere di latte _____ un panino.
h _____ il freddo che faceva ho dovuto comprarmi un
   berretto di lana.

Exercise 57 (Unit 74)

Re-write the sentences with the preposition *di* if it is needed.

E.g. un paio scarpe → un paio di scarpe

a un vestito seta
b un bicchiere rotto
c un bicchiere vino
d Il mio giardino è più piccolo tuo.
e Hai visto niente interessante?
f Sono inglese.
g Soffre gotta (*gout*).

h la città romana
i la città Firenze
j Ti consiglio scrivergli.
k un tavolo legno
l la scrivania Giorgio
m Ho deciso venire.
n Sono Londra.

Exercise 58 (Unit 75)

Write the missing prepositions *con*, *di* and *a* in the blanks. In some cases you will need to combine them with the article. Then read the passage aloud slowly and clearly.

Quando vado in Italia, visito sempre nuovi posti. Due anni fa sono andata in Toscana: a _____ Siena, b _____ Lucca, c _____ Vinci e d _____ isola d'Elba. Quando ero e _____ Siena ho fatto un'escursione f _____ Monteriggioni, una cittadina costruita nel 1200 sulla cima g _____ una collina e circondata da mura h _____ quattordici torrioni. i _____ Lucca ho visitato la casa j _____ Puccini, il compositore k _____ 'Boheme'. l _____ Vinci sono stata m _____ Museo Leonardiano. n _____ isola d'Elba sono stata o _____ Marciana Alta e da lì, p _____ la funivia (*cable car*), sono salita fino q _____ Monte Capanne da dove si gode una vista bellissima.

Exercise 59 (Unit 76)

Translate the following into Italian.
a When I am in Italy, I often go to Tuscany.
b When I used to live in Cornwall, I used to go to France every year.
c I have not decided whether (**se**) to go to Sicily or to Elba.
d I live in town.
e This afternoon I am going to town.
f My sister went to live in the country.
g The Simoni family is in the mountains.
h Francesco is jogging (**sta facendo il jogging**) in the park.
i My Italian course starts in winter.
j In 2006 I will go to Australia.
k My train arrived on time.
l I take my holidays in the summer.

Exercise 60 (Unit 77)

Fill the blanks with the expressions from the box.
Non mi sembra che mio figlio studi a _____ . Nove volte
b _____ ritorna a casa con un brutto voto. Anche in classe
è svogliato e disattento, infatti il suo professore mi ha detto
che ieri era c _____ di mandarlo fuori. Nella prova scritta
di francese ha commesso d _____ . Nonostante mi faccia
e _____ di studiare di più, non riesce a migliorare.

> promesse su promesse   errori su errori   sul punto
> sul serio   su dieci

Exercise 61 (Unit 78)

Add the appropriate expressions from the box to complete the dialogue below.

'Hai **a** _____ visto Margherita? **b** _____ arriva **c** _____ . Non riesco a capire perché sia tanto in ritardo.'

'Ah, sì, l'ho vista per le scale due ore fa. Stava andando a fare le pulizie dalla signora del piano di sopra.'

'Ho capito, si vede che non (*she mustn't*) ha ancora (*yet*) finito.'

'**d** _____ la signora del piano di sopra la fa lavorare troppo. È una famiglia di persone per bene ma sono un po' tirchi (*stingy*).'

'**e** _____ Margherita non si è mai lamentata.'

'**f** _____ : Margherita non si lamenta mai e la gente se ne approfitta (*take advantage of her*).'

'**g** _____ c'è gente molto altruista come la famiglia Marchese che le fa tanti regali.'

'Altruista per modo di dire, perché qualche volta si dimenticano di pagarla. **h** _____ non le pagano nemmeno le marche (*stamps*) per la pensione.'

'Mamma mia, che gente meschina (*mean*)!'

'**i** _____ !'

per fortuna	per di più	Per l'appunto!
per lo più	per tempo	per me	per quanto io sappia
	per caso	per l'appunto

Exercise 62 (Unit 79)

Yesterday the teacher took his class to the cinema, and this morning the children had to write about the film. This is Marietto's essay. Unfortunately he left out most of the prepositions, some of them with an article – add them for him.

IL FILM

Il ladro uscì a _____ casa b _____ un'anziana signora correndo verso (*toward*) il bosco. Il chiarore c _____ luna che filtrava d _____ i rami gli permetteva e _____ vedere appena (*just*) il sentiero che portava f _____ città. g _____ frattempo l'anziana signora, che durante la rapina si era nascosta tremante sotto (*under*) il letto, corse h _____ telefono i _____ chiamare la polizia e scorse, j _____ le tende socchiuse, la figura k _____ uomo che, uscito dalla boscaglia, correva verso la città dove si svolgeva una grande festa religiosa l _____ la banda locale e i fuochi d'artificio. Il ladro fu trovato m _____ la folla ed arrestato. La vecchia signora venne a sapere che il ladro aveva rubato n _____ salvare la sua famiglia da una vita piena di tribolazioni e che si era pentito. La signora decise di perdonarlo e cominciò o _____ andarlo a trovare in prigione e, p _____ una visita e l'altra, andava anche a trovare la sua povera famiglia q _____ tantissimi doni, cibo e giocattoli. Il giorno r _____ cui l'uomo uscì s _____ prigione andò t _____ attenderlo e lo portò u _____ sua grande casa v _____ tutta la sua povera famiglia. L'uomo diventò giardiniere ed autista w _____ signora e sua moglie cuoca.

Exercise 63 (Unit 80)

Fill the blanks using *da, dal, dall', dallo* etc.

a Domani andrò _____ Andrea.

b A che ora parte il treno _____ Milano?

c Devo andare _____ fruttivendolo.

d Ho bisogno di un servizio _____ caffè.

e _____ quanto tempo abiti in Francia?

f Abito in Francia _____ '73.

g Non vedo Mario _____ un mese.

h Non ho niente _____ dichiarare.

i Alle tre esco _____ università.

j Siamo qui _____ pochi giorni

Exercise 64 (Unit 81)

Choose a word or expression from the box to complete the sentences.

> tramite   nonostante   invece di   durante   circa
>
> senza   assieme a

a _____ tutto è sempre molto contento.

b L'ho vista passare _____ suo marito.

c Ho mandato il pacco _____ il corriere.

d _____ guardare la TV, perché non esci?

e Non devi attraversare la strada _____ ben guardare prima a sinistra, poi a destra, poi ancora a sinistra.

f _____ l'estate arrivano i turisti.

g Avrà _____ cinquant'anni.

Exercise 65 (Unit 82)

Choose a suitable adverb from the box for each sentence.

> costantemente impulsivamente terribilmente precipitosamente
> attivamente vigorosamente allegramente confusamente

a Marietto non riesce a tacere (*to be quiet*) un momento: parla
_____ . **b** Gli studenti uscirono dall'aula _____ .
c Partecipa _____ a molte opere di beneficenza. **d** Negò
tutto _____ . **e** Agì _____ . **f** Ha preso lo scherzo _____ .
g Il discorso è stato _____ noioso. **h** A causa del buio
vedeva _____ .

Exercise 66 (Unit 83)

**Translate into Italian the adverb or adverbial expressions in
this dialogue between Marcella and her friend Elisa.**

MARCELLA Non riesco a trovare il
gatto, ho guardato (**a**
everywhere): (**b** *under*) il
sofà, (**c** *up there*),
sull'armadio, (**d** *outside*),
ma non lo trovo.

ELISA Sarà (**e** *somewhere else*).
Non ti preoccupare, lo
sai che (**f** *every so often*)
scompare.

MARCELLA Sì lo so, ma (**g** *usually*) scompare dopo aver mangiato. Non va (**h** *never*) via a stomaco vuoto. Non può essere andato tanto (**i** *far*).

ELISA Quando lo hai visto, l'ultima volta?

MARCELLA Mah, saranno state le otto …

ELISA Sarà (**j** *upstairs*).

MARCELLA Non credo perché sono scesa proprio (**k** *now*) e non l'ho visto.

ELISA (**l** *Then*) potrebbe essere dalla vicina, lo sai che al suo bambino piace giocare con lui.

MARCELLA (**m** *Perhaps*). Vado a vedere e torno (**n** *immediately*) perché il pollo al forno è (**o** *nearly*) pronto.
(*after a little while*)

MARCELLA Non è (**p** *not even there*). Pazienza, vado un momento (**q** *upstairs*) e poi pranziamo.
(*a few moments later*)

MARCELLA Avevi ragione. il gatto è (**r** *upstairs*) (**s** *under*) la poltrona e si sta mangiando il pollo!

Exercise 67 (Unit 85)

Combine the sentences using the conjunctions in bold which follow each one.

a Questa mattina ho deciso di prendere il battello per Vernazza.
Fa bel tempo. Il mare è calmo. **perché e**

b Generalmente arrivo presto alla stazione marittima. Mi piace sedere a prora. Non sempre ci riesco. La gente, anche se arriva dopo di me, riesce sempre a salire prima. Durante il viaggio immagino di essere sola sul mio panfilo.   **poiché ma siccome mentre**

c All'arrivo mi fermo sulla piccola spiaggia. Vado al bar a prendere un succo di frutta.   **oppure**

d Verso le quattro e mezzo è ora di tornare. Salgo sul battello. **quindi**

e Una giornata tranquilla. Non noiosa. Molto benefica. Fisicamente. Per la mente.   **ma anzi sia che**

Exercise 68 (Unit 86)

Translate the following into Italian.

a Although she doesn't say it, she would like to go to the mountains.

b Despite the fact that he has won the lottery, he lives as before.

c She is always very cheerful, as long as one does not mention Bruno.

d You must book (**prenotare**) the hotel before it's too late.

e If you need something, you must let me know.

f Unless you work, you cannot buy that boat (**barca**).

g I think she has arrived.

h He bought this flat (**appartamento**) without my knowlege.

Exercise 69 (Unit 87)

Match the two halves of the sentences.

a Quando eravamo in Italia
siamo andati a trovarli ...

b Me lo hanno fatto pagare
il doppio.

c Per amor del cielo,...

d Mamma mia, ...

e Povero me, ...

f Evviva, ...

g Coraggio, ...

h Su, ...

i Uffa, ...

j Ehi, ...

1 ... dico a te! Sei sordo?

2 ... che barba!

3 ... fai presto!

4 ... che presto arriva l'ambulanza!

5 ... la nostra squadra ha vinto!

6 ... ho perso il passaporto!

7 ... che carattere che hai!

8 ... non dirle nulla!

9 ... Che fregatura!

10 ... ma, ahimè, loro erano
in Francia!

Exercise 70 (Unit 88)

Match the questions and answers.

a Dove andrete in vacanza per
il ferragosto?

b Hai fatto il compito?

c Quanto hai pagato questo vestito?

d Io non ci credo, e tu?

e Che cosa ti ha detto Teresa?

f Chi di voi ha preso la mia auto?

g Faresti il paracadutista?

h Hai visto Mario o Goffredo?

1 Neanch'io (*Nor do I*).

2 Niente, l'ho fatto io.

3 No.

4 Nessuno.

5 Mai!

6 Né l'uno né l'altro.

7 Da nessuna parte.

8 Niente.

Exercise 71 (Unit 89)

Add *a meno che non* **+ subjunctive to the sentences below.**

E.g. Concluderò l'affare _____ (esserci) problemi finanziari. →
Concluderò l'affare a meno che non ci siano problemi
finanziari.

a Uscirò _____ (piovere).

b Arriveranno in ritardo _____ (partire) presto.

c Verrà questa sera _____ (essere) chiamato d'urgenza
all'ospedale.

d Andrò col treno delle nove _____ ce ne (essere) uno prima.

e Ti aspetterò _____ tu (arrivare) in ritardo.

f Comprerò quell'auto _____ (essere) troppo cara.

Exercise 72 (Unit 90)

Modify the sentences below using *il/la* **etc.** *cui* **+ noun.**

E.g. Lo scrittore, i libri del quale sono tanto apprezzati, ha
cambiato lavoro.
→ Lo scrittore, i cui libri sono tanto apprezzati, ha
cambiato lavoro.

a La casa, il proprietario della quale è stato arrestato, è in vendita.

b Il cane, il proprietario del quale è all'ospedale, è rimasto solo.

c Maria, il marito della quale ha vinto al lotto, vuole divorziare.

d Il cantante, i dischi del quale vanno a ruba (*sell like hot cakes*),
terrà un concerto al Teatro Regio.

e Il giornalista, l'articolo del quale è tanto discusso, è stato
denunciato.

f Gli studenti, il professore dei quali ha l'influenza, sono
felicissimi.

Exercise 73 (Unit 91)

Match the two halves of the sentences.

a Ciò che fai …   1 … è falso.
b Quello che dici mi …   2 … sembra giusto.
c Ciò che conta …   3 … non m'interessa.
d Tutto quello che so è …   4 … è essere sereni.
e Tutto quello che dice …   5 … che c'è qualcosa che
                                              non va.
f Tutto quello che fa è …   6 … mangiare e dormire.
g Con tutto quello che guadagna …   7 … non ha mai una lira.
h Per tutto quello che ha fatto …   8 … ha ricevuto un premio.

Exercise 74 (Unit 92)

Translate into Italian.

a Would you like another one? (*feminine*)
b Each one of them had their share (**la sua parte**).
c Many believe in this medicine.
d Quite a lot of them were annoyed (**seccati**).
e Is there anyone who wants a slice (**fetta**) of cake?
f No one said anything.
g A few think that it is (*subjunctive*) possible.
h She is capable of anything.

Exercise 75 (Unit 94)

Translate into Italian.

a Excuse me, madam, what did you say?
b What is your name (sir)?

c How long have you been living in Brighton?
d What is your cousin Giacomo like?
e How long will they go on like that?
f How long does it take you (*inf., sing.*) to get dressed?
g How often do you go to the theatre?
h How come you never tell the truth (**verità**)?
i Why on earth do you want to wear such a (**un tale**) dress?

Exercise 76 (Unit 95)

Translate the following into Italian.

a What kind of coffee do you want madam?
b What kinds do you (*inf. sing.*) have?
c What is the matter with you, madam?
d What's on at the Ritz?
e Whose turn is it?
f Whose shoes are these?
g What time is the train to Milan?
h What's the time?
i Where do they come from?
j What do you want it for?

Exercise 77 (Unit 96)

Fill the blanks to complete each sentence.

a Abbiamo una _____ da cento grammi e una da duecento grammi. Quale vuole?
b A Milano deve cambiare e prendere la _____ delle tre per Caronno.

c Vai a prendere il vino in _____ .
d A mezzogiorno mangio alla _____ .
e A Carnevale si usa gettare _____ alla gente che passa.
f _____ un attimo (*moment*) prego, vado a chiamarlo.
g Io vi ho _____ ; poi fate come volete.
h Cambiamo _____ di conversazione, se non vi dispiace.
i _____ un corso d'italiano all'università di Brighton.
j Ecco la _____ _____ . Fammi una foto.
k Cerca di non offenderlo, è un ragazzo molto _____ .
l I miei _____ si sono sposati 25 anni fa.

1 a La mamma prepara il pasto per il bambino.
b I libri che ho ordinato arriveranno la settimana prossima.
c Il treno dell 6.45 (sei e quarantacinque) arriverà presto.
d Mariella scrive una lettera.

2 Suggested answers: Francesco è un cantante
famoso./Elisa legge un libro interessante./Filippo ha
un'automobile enorme./Mario indossa un vestito blu.

3 a il mal di denti **b** — **c** il mal di testa **d** il mal di
cuore **e** il Mar Adriatico **f** un cuor d'oro **g** qual è?
h sta' attento **i** un po' di vino

4 a aereo (*m.*) **b** moto(cicletta) (*f.*) **c** cane (*m.*)
d mano (*f.*) **e** auto(mobile) (*f.*) **f** radio (*f.*)

5 Nouns with an -**h** in the plural: buchi, banche

6 a viaggi **b** figli **c** zii **d** leggii **e** specchi **f** brusii

7 a Parla francese? Studia il francese? **b** Parla inglese?
Studia l'inglese? **c** Parla tedesco? Studia il tedesco?
d Parla spagnolo? Studia lo spagnolo? **e** Parla greco?
Studia il greco? **f** Parla portoghese? Studia il portoghese?
g Parla turco? Studia il turco? **h** Parla arabo? Studia
l'arabo? **i** Parla russo? Studia il russo? **j** Parla olandese?
Studia l'olandese? **k** Parla polacco? Studia il polacco?
l Parla danese? Studia il danese? **m** Parla svedese? Studia
lo svedese? **n** Parla norvegese? Studia il norvegese?
o Parla finlandese? Studia il finlandese?

8 a Il vino Soave costa quattro euro e cinquanta al litro.
b Mi piace vedere/guardare il calcio alla TV. **c** Il novanta
per cento della popolazione ha l'automobile. **d** Una lezione
costa venticinque sterline all'ora. **e** la Roma Imperiale
f La cena è pronta. **g** A che ora è la colazione?

9 a Che peccato! **b** mezzo chilo di mele **c** mezz'ora
d cento volte **e** sei ore al giorno **f** due volte al giorno
g mezza pinta **h** Che bel ragazzo! **i** Ho mal di gola.
j Ho mal di testa. **k** Andrea ha mal di denti. **l** Goffredo
ha il raffreddore. **m** Angela ha un raffreddore terribile.
n Ho una fretta! **o** Ho un appetito! **p** Da bambina ero
un maschiaccio.

10 a l'arco **b** una radio **c** Il tasso **d** Il manico **e** un
foglio **f** La posta **g** tappo **h** la capitale **i** le tappe
j una foglia

11 Masculine nouns: e, g, h, m, p, q, r, v; Feminine nouns:
b, c, i, k, n, o, t, u; Common gender nouns: a, d, f, j, l, s.

12 a la donna **b** il fratello **c** il marito **d** la nubile
e il genero **f** la femmina **g** le qualità **h** le quantità
i le virtù **j** le città **k** i caffè **l** i tè

13 un miglio **b** due miglia **c** un centinaio di persone
d dieci dita **e** un migliaio di dollari **f** alcune migliaia di
miglia **g** un dito

14 a un donnone e un ometto **b** un tavolino **c** un
omaccio

15 a capolavori **b** capoversi **c** capogiri **d** capigruppo
e capisquadra **f** capitecnici **g** capistazione **h** capifila

16 a 13 **b** 19 **c** 16 **d** 12 **e** 2 **f** 9 **g** 17 **h** 3
i 8 **j** 18 **k** 10 **l** 1 **m** 4 **n** 20 **o** 21 **p** 22
q 14 **r** 15 **s** 7 **t** 5 **u** 11 **v** 6

17 a Voglio questo. **b** Prendo questi. **c** Non voglio
quello. **d** Non prendo quelle.

18 Suggested answers: **a** Devo pagare il lattaio ogni
settimana. **b** Devo pagare la bolletta del telefono ogni tre
mesi. **c** Devo pagare la tassa di circolazione ogni anno.
d Devo pagare la segretaria ogni mese.

19 a i nostri **b** la loro **c** Il mio **d** (i) suoi; (i) miei
e la mia **f** il suo **g** Il tuo **h** I suoi

20 a 1 **b** 4 **c** 6 **d** 3 **e** 2 **f** 5

21 a Papa Paolo Sesto **b** Pio Nono **c** Leone Decimo
d Giovanni Ventitreesimo **e** Giovanni Paolo Secondo
f Re Vittorio Emanuele Terzo **g** Gustavo Sedicesimo
h Giorgio Sesto **i** Enrico Quarto **j** Regina Elisabetta
Seconda

22 a Secondo alcuni, il terzo millennio va dal primo
gennaio duemila al trentun dicembre duemilanovecento-
novantanove. **b** Dante è il grande poeta del Duecento.
c L'attuale secolo si chiama il ventunesimo secolo.

23 a un mezzo **b** due terzi **c** tre quarti **d** cinque ottavi **e** sette ottavi **f** quattro quinti **g** cinque sedicesimi **h** diciannove trentaduesimi **i** cinque sesti **j** nove decimi **k** Cinque più dodici fa diciassette. **l** Dieci meno sei fa quattro. **m** Dieci per dieci fa cento. **n** Dodici diviso due fa sei. **o** Quarantacinque meno trenta fa quindici. **p** Centoventicinque per settantacinque fa novemilatrecentosettantacinque. **q** Centotrentasei diviso cinque fa ventisette virgola due. **r** Quattrocentocinquant-uno diviso otto fa cinquantasei virgola trentasette.

24 Individual responses.

25 a sale **b** saliamo **c** tengono **d** spengono **e** spengo **f** tieni **g** tengono **h** teniamo **i** scegliete **j** rimango **k** scelgono **l** rimani

26 a Rispondo io! **b** Rispondi tu? **c** Risponde lui? **d** Compri tu le cartoline? **e** Comprate voi le cartoline? **f** Sì, compriamo noi le cartoline.

27 a preso **b** prese **c** comprata **d** venduta

28 a Voglio vederlo. **b** Voglio parlargli. **c** Voglio telefonarle. **d** Devo scrivervi. **e** Deve vederci. **f** Devo leggerlo. **g** Posso vederlo? **h** Posso telefonargli? **i** Puoi scriverci?

29 a C'è un supermercato qui vicino? **b** Ci vado ogni mese/tutti i mesi. **c** Ci vengo una volta all'anno. **d** Ci pensiamo sempre. **e** Ci sono sette giorni in una settimana.

30 a Sì, è in discoteca. **b** Sì, sono in classe. **c** Sì, è in banca. **d** Sì, sono italiani. **e** No, non sei alla partita. **f** No, non siamo a Capri. **g** No, non sono a casa. **h** No, non sono alla mensa.

31 a 1 **b** 3 **c** 4 **d** 6 **e** 5 **f** 7 **g** 2

32 a Fa molto caldo. **b** Roberta fa le valigie. **c** Loro fanno i biglietti.

33 a danno **b** dai **c** danno **d** dà/dai **e** sai; so **f** sa **g** so

34 a Come sta, signora? **b** Dove sta? **c** non sta mai fermo. **d** Come stai/sta?

35 a 5 **b** 7 **c** 8 **d** 4 **e** 6 **f** 2 **g** 3 **h** 1

36 a venuto **b** rotto **c** offerto **d** corso **e** fatto **f** messo **g** bevuto **h** preso **i** visto **j** rimasto **k** aperto **l** stato **m** chiuso **n** scritto **o** nato **p** mosso **q** letto **r** detto **s** sceso **t** vissuto

37 a Sono stato in vacanza con Claire. **b** Abbiamo preso il battello per San Fruttuoso. **c** Abbiamo camminato tutto il giorno. **d** Abbiamo fatto un po' di spesa. **e** Siamo andati in discoteca. **f** Abbiamo bevuto un caffè e siamo usciti. **g** Hanno preso il treno. **h** Sono tornati a casa la settimana scorsa. **i** È arrivata a Portofino. **j** Il ladro è scappato.

38 **a** abitavano **b** iniziavano **c** andavo **d** era **e** c'era **f** si poteva **g** c'erano **h** Bastava **i** si vedeva **j** era **k** c'era **l** vendeva **m** si vedeva **n** conduceva **o** potevano **p** c'era **q** andavano **r** si sentivano **s** giocavo **t** osservavo **u** si scaldavano

39 **a** Ne bastano due cucchiaini. **b** Ne basta mezzo bicchiere. **c** Ne bastano cento grammi **d** No, basta studiare. **e** No, basta avere la carta stradale.

40 **A Cristina** **a** non piace il calcio. **b** piace suonare il pianoforte. **c** non piacciono i cioccolatini. **d** piace la musica. **A Marco** **a** piace guardare la televisione. **b** piace la/andare in motocicletta. **c** non piacciono i dolci. **d** non piace la frutta.

41 **a** nuoterò **b** mi abbronzerò **c** leggerò **d** farò **e** prenderò **f** scriverò **g** non guarderò **h** non leggerò

42 **a** Vorrei una birra e un panino. **b** Mi piacerebbe andare in vacanza. **c** Dovresti dirglielo. **d** Non potrei farlo. **e** Non lo farebbe.

43 **a** Scrivigliela. **b** Raccontaglielo. **c** Gliela venda. **d** Glielo compri. **e** Glielo consigli. **f** Parlategliene. **g** Mandateglieli. *Negative*: **a** Non scrivere la lettera a Marcello. **b** Non raccontare tutto a Goffredo. **c** Non venda la macchina a Susanna. **d** Non compri un nuovo computer a Sandro. **e** Non consigli a Renzo di stare a

casa.   **f** Non parlate del fatto al presidente.
g Non mandate i documenti al sindaco.

44 a abbiano comprato **b** abbia meritato **c** abbia
mangiato **d** abbia avuto **e** abbia venduto

45 a 6 **b** 5 **c** 3 **d** 7 **e** 4 **f** 8 **g** 2 **h** 1

46 a 3 **b** 5 **c** 2 **d** 1 **e** 6 **f** 4

47 a Voglio che tu esca di più. **b** Credo che vogliano
cambiare casa. **c** Pensavo che venisse. **d** Penso che lo/la
tenga nella scrivania. **e** Se dovessero scegliere andrebbero
in Francia.

48 a nacque **b** fu **c** ritornò **d** ritornò **e** ritirò
f visse

49 a Non essendo stanco è andato a piedi. **b** Essendo
chiusi i negozi è andato al ristorante. **c** Avendo comprato
i biglietti sono tornato a casa. **d** Avendo commesso tale
gaffe preferì tacere per il resto della serata.
e Attraversando la strada inciampò e cadde. **f** Uscendo di
casa decise di prendere l'ombrello.

50 a Francesco è un dirigente importante. **b** Durante il
secolo scorso molti emigranti italiani andarono in America.
c Ambedue i contendenti sono molto bravi. **d** È un mio
conoscente. **e** La mia lavatrice non funziona. **f** Voglio
una nuova canna da pesca per Natale.

51 a Vanno a nuotare ogni giorno. **b** Marianna e Paolo vanno a pescare quando possono. **c** Sono stanco(-a) di ripetere le stesse cose. **d** Non sono riusciti a convincerlo.

52 a produce; prodotta **b** posto; poste **c** trae; traggono; esposto; espongono

53 a 7 **b** 8 **c** 6 **d** 1 **e** 2 **f** 3 **g** 4 **h** 5

54 Individual responses.

55 a di **b** a **c** a **d** a **e** a **f** a **g** a **h** al **i** ad **j** di **k** di **l** a **m** a **n** di **o** a **p** di

56 a ad **b** di **c** con **d** a **e** con **f** con **g** con **h** Con

57 a un vestito di seta **b** un bicchiere rotto **c** un bicchiere di vino **d** Il mio giardino è più piccolo del tuo. **e** Hai visto niente di interessante? **f** Sono inglese. **g** Soffre di gotta. **h** la città romana **i** la città di Firenze **j** Ti consiglio di scrivergli. **k** un tavolo di legno **l** la scrivania di Giorgio **m** Ho deciso di venire. **n** Sono di Londra.

58 a a **b** a **c** a **d** all' **e** a **f** a **g** di **h** con **i** A **j** di **k** della **l** A **m** al **n** All' **o** a **p** con **q** al

59 a Quando sono in Italia vado spesso in Toscana. **b** Quando vivevo in Cornovaglia andavo in Francia ogni anno. **c** Non ho deciso se andare in Sicilia o all'isola d'Elba. **d** Vivo/Abito in città. **e** Questo pomeriggio vado in città. **f** Mia sorella è andata a vivere in campagna. **g** La famiglia Simoni è/I Simoni sono in montagna. **h** Francesco sta facendo il jogging nel parco. **i** Il mio corso d'italiano comincia in/d'inverno. **j** Nel 2006 andrò in Australia. **k** Il mio treno è arrivato in orario. **l** Vado in vacanza in/d'estate.

60 **a** sul serio **b** su dieci **c** sul punto **d** errori su errori **e** promesse su promesse

61 **a** per caso **b** per lo più **c** per tempo **d** Per me **e** Per quanto io sappia **f** Per l'appunto **g** Per fortuna **h** Per di più **i** Per l'appunto!

62 **a** dalla **b** di **c** della **d** tra **e** di **f** in **g** Nel **h** al **i** per **j** tra **k** dell' **l** con **m** tra **n** per **o** ad **p** tra **q** con **r** in **s** di **t** ad **u** nella **v** con **w** della

63 **a** da **b** da **c** dal **d** da **e** Da **f** dal **g** da **h** da **i** dall' **j** da

64 **a** Nonostante **b** assieme a **c** tramite **d** Invece di **e** senza **f** Durante **g** circa

65 **a** costantemente **b** precipitosamente **c** attivamente **d** vigorosamente **e** impulsivamente **f** allegramente **g** terribilmente **h** confusamente

66 **a** dappertutto **b** sotto **c** lassù **d** fuori **e** altrove
f ogni tanto **g** di solito **h** mai **i** lontano **j** di sopra
k adesso/ora **l** Allora **m** Forse **n** immediatamente
o quasi **p** neppure là **q** di sopra **r** di sopra **s** sotto

67 **a** Questa mattina ho deciso di prendere il battello per
Vernazza perché fa bel tempo e il mare è calmo.
b Generalmente arrivo presto alla stazione marittima poiché
mi piace sedere a prora ma non sempre ci riesco siccome la
gente, anche se arriva dopo di me, riesce sempre a salire
prima. Mentre viaggio immagino di essere sola sul mio
panfilo. **c** All'arrivo mi fermo sulla piccola spiaggia
oppure vado al bar a prendere un succo di frutta. **d** Verso
le quattro e mezzo è ora di tornare, quindi salgo sul battello.
e Una giornata tranquilla ma non noiosa, anzi, molto
benefica sia fisicamente che per la mente.

68 **a** Benché non lo dica, vorrebbe andare in montagna.
b Nonostante (il fatto che) abbia vinto alla lotteria, vive
come prima. **c** È sempre molto contenta a patto che non
si parli di Bruno. **d** Devi prenotare l'albergo prima che sia
troppo tardi. **e** Nel caso che tu avessi bisogno di qualcosa,
devi farmelo sapere. **f** A meno che tu non lavori, non puoi
comprare quella barca. **g** Penso che sia arrivata. **h** Ha
comprato questo appartamento senza che io lo sapessi.

69 **a** 10 **b** 9 **c** 8 **d** 7 **e** 6 **f** 5 **g** 4 **h** 3
i 2 **j** 1

70 a 7 b 3 c 2 d 1 e 8 f 4 g 5 h 6

71 a a meno che non piova b a meno che non partano
c a meno che non sia d a meno che non ce ne sia e a
meno che tu non arrivi f a meno che non sia

72 a La casa, il cui proprietario è stato arrestato, è in
vendita. b Il cane, il cui proprietario è all'ospedale, è
rimasto solo. c Maria, il cui marito ha vinto al lotto,
vuole divorziare. d Il cantante i cui dischi vanno a ruba,
terrà un concerto al Teatro Regio. e Il giornalista, il cui
articolo è tanto discusso, è stato denunciato. f Gli
studenti, il cui professore ha l'influenza, sono felicissimi.

73 a 3 b 2 c 4 d 5 e 1 f 6 g 7 h 8

74 a Ne vorresti/vorrebbe un'altra? b Ciascuno di loro
ha avuto la sua parte. c Molti credono in questa
medicina. d Non pochi di loro erano seccati. e C'è
qualcuno che vuole una fetta di torta? f Nessuno ha detto
niente. g Pochi pensano che sia possibile. h È capace di
tutto. È capace di qualunque/qualsiasi cosa.

75 a Scusi signora, che cosa ha detto? b Come si chiama,
signore? c Da quanto tempo abiti/abita a Brighton?
d Com'è tuo/suo cugino Giacomo? e Fino a quando
continueranno così? f Quanto tempo (ti) ci vuole per
vestirti? g Ogni quanto/Quante volte vai/va a teatro?
h Come mai non dici/dice mai la verità? i Perché mai
vuoi mettere/indossare un tale vestito?

76 a Che tipo di caffè desidera/vuole, Signora?
b Che tipi ha? **c** Che cosa le succede, signora? **d** Che
cosa danno al Ritz? **e** A chi tocca? **f** Di chi sono queste
scarpe? **g** A che ora è il treno per Milano? **h** Che ore
sono? **i** Da dove vengono? **j** Perché/A che scopo lo
vuole/vuoi?

77 a confezione **b** coincidenza **c** cantina **d** mensa
e coriandoli **f** Attenda **g** avvisato **h** argomento
i Frequento **j** macchina fotografica **k** sensibile
l genitori

This section is intended for those readers who may not be familiar with all the grammar terms in this book.

accents In Italian, accents are placed on a few vowels which need to be pronounced with a stress when they occur at the end of a word. The vowel e is the only vowel which can carry either a grave accent (è) or an acute accent (é). In the former case it is pronounced as in *well* and in the latter as in *they*. The vowels a, i, o, and u normally only have a grave accent: à, ì, ò and ù.

active The most common form of a verb which occurs when the subject carries out the action of the verb: *Sting sings the song*. (See also passive.)

adjectives Words used to describe a noun. These can be:
  descriptive *beautiful, red, large, easy, sad, happy*, etc.
  demonstrative *this book, that car, these books, those cars*
  indefinite *every time, some books, each room*
  possessive *her desk, his umbrella, their car*
  interrogative *which car? how much sugar? how many cars?*
  comparative (expressing a comparison): *more ... than, less ... than, as ... as*
  superlative *the most, the least*

adverbs Words which modify a verb: *Paul plays well*. They can also modify an adjective: *Paul is very handsome*, or another adverb: *Paul plays very well*.

conjunctions Words connecting other words, clauses or sentences: *bread and butter, slowly but surely, I'll go if they ask me*.

conjugation A verb is conjugated when it is formed into its various forms of mood, tense and person. The present tense of essere (*to be*) is conjugated as follows:

sono	sei	è	siamo	siete	sono
I am	*you are*	*s/he it is*	*we are*	*you (pl.) are*	*they are*

'false friends' Words which look like other words in a different language, but which have a completely different meaning.

gerund A verb mood. English words ending in -*ing* are most often gerunds: *coming, living.*

impersonal verbs Verbs without a specific subject. They are only used in the third person singular: *It is said that he is very rich.*

infinitive The mood of the verb which merely expresses its meaning without saying who is carrying out the action nor when the action is occurring: *to go, to say, to do.* In Italian, the infinitive is expressed by one word, usually ending in -are, -ere or -ire: andare, vedere, dire. A few infinitives end in -urre, -orre or -arre.

intransitive Verbs normally used without an object (i.e. the action of the subject doesn't transit to the object): *It's raining.* Sometimes a verb can be used both transitively and intransitively: *He eats* (what?) *a roll* is transitive. *He eats at seven* is intransitive. (See also **transitive**.)

invariable A word that doesn't change its form.

moods The manner in which the action is carried out: whether it is really happening or has happened or is going to happen (indicative mood = *I speak/I spoke/I was speaking/I will speak*, etc.), whether it is an order or suggestion (imperative mood = *go!*), whether it depends on a condition (conditional mood = *I would if I could*), whether it is only probable or a wish (subjunctive mood = *I wish I were rich*, etc.).

nouns Words used for naming people (*Carla*), animals (*giraffe*), objects (*table*), places (*Italy*), and concepts (*beauty*), the latter being called an **abstract noun**. They can be **singular** or **plural** (usually referred to as **number**) and – in Italian – they have a **gender**, either **masculine** or **feminine**. The gender can be found in the dictionary (*m.* or *f.*) but most often it can be recognized by the noun's ending or by the article which precedes it.

object The person, animal, being or thing undergoing the action carried out by the subject.

passive The form of a verb where the grammatical subject has the action done to it, instead of doing the action itself: *The song is sung by Sting*. (See also **active**.)

person Refers to (a) the person(s) speaking (1st person singular or plural: *I* or *we*); (b) the person(s) or thing(s) spoken to (2nd person singular or plural: *you*); (c) the person(s) or thing(s) spoken of (3rd person singular of plural: *he/she/it* or *they*).

prepositions Used to mark the relation of a word with another, in space (*on, under, below, near, in front of* etc.) or time (*before, after,* etc.). In Italian they can be **simple** (e.g. *di* = *of*) or **combined** (with the definite article, e.g. *of the* = **del/dello/della/dell'/dei/degli/delle**).

pronouns Words used to replace the noun or the name of a person in order not to repeat it. There are several kinds of pronouns.

subject pronouns *I, you, he/she/it, we, you (plural), they*; these denote the person or subject carrying out the action of the verb: *I am writing a book.*

object pronouns Denote the object of the verb. They can be **direct:** *me, you, him/her/it, us, you* (pl.), *them* (e.g. *I see them*) or **indirect:** *to me, to him/to her/to it, to us, to you* (pl.), *to them*: *I gave the book to them.*

NOTE Although in English you can say *I gave them a book, them* in this case is really *to them* and is therefore an indirect object pronoun.

pronouns preceded by a preposition (other than *to*). Also known as **disjunctive pronouns** *for me, by him,* etc.

reflexive pronouns *myself, yourself, him/herself,* etc. are so called because they are used as the object of reflexive verbs: *I wash myself.*

possessive pronouns *mine, yours, theirs,* etc.

relative pronouns *who, whom, which, that, whose.*

interrogative pronouns *Who? Whom? What? Which (ones)?,* etc.

demonstrative pronouns *this (one), these (ones),* etc.: *I'll take this one.*

reflexive verbs Verbs that express an action which reflects back to the subject: *I wash myself.*

subject The being or thing carrying out the action of the verb: *I read the book* (the book 'receives' the action of my reading it). (See also **pronouns** and **passive**.)

syllable Each individual sound which makes up a word: *bi-cy-cle*.

tense Indicates the time during which something is happening: *I speak/I am speaking* = **present** (*speaking*) = **gerund**); *I spoke* = **past**; *I will speak* = **future**; *I have spoken* = **perfect** (*spoken* = **past participle**).

transitive Verbs where the action passes from the subject to the object: *We sold the house*. (See also **intransitive**.)

verbs Indicate the action or the state of a person, animal or thing.

Numbers refer to the units of the grammar.

teach yourself

beginner's italian
vittoria bowles

- Are you new to language learning?
- Do you want lots of practice and examples?
- Do you want to improve your confidence to speak?

Beginner's Italian is written for the complete beginner who
wants to move at a steady pace and have lots of opportunity
to practise. The grammar is explained clearly and does not
assume that you have studied a language before. You will
learn everything you need to get the most out of a holiday or
to go on to further study.

italian verbs
maria bonacina

- Do you want a handy reference to check verb forms?
- Are you finding tenses difficult?
- Do you want to see verbs used in a variety of contexts?

Italian Verbs is a quick and easy way to check the form and meaning of over 3500 verbs. The clear layout makes the book very easy to navigate and the examples make the uses clear at the same time as building your vocabulary.